MAKE INK

for all my mothers

Editors: John Gall and Ashley Albert
Designers: John Gall and Najeebah Al-Ghadban
Production Manager: Anet Sirna-Bruder

Library of Congress Control Number: 2017956855

ISBN: 978-1-4197-3243-0
eISBN: 978-1-68335-327-0

Text Copyright © 2018 Jason Logan
Photographs Copyright © 2018 Lauren Kolyn

Cover © 2018 Abrams

Printed and bound in China
12

Abrams books are available at special discounts when
purchased in quantity for premiums and promotions as
well as fundraising or educational use. Special editions
can also be created to specification. For details, contact
specialsales@abramsbooks.com or the address below.

Abrams® is a registered trademark of Harry N. Abrams, Inc.

ABRAMS The Art of Books
195 Broadway, New York, NY 10007
abramsbooks.com

MAKE INK

JASON LOGAN

Conversation with Michael Ondaatje

Photography by Lauren Kolyn

Abrams, New York

CONTENTS

FOREWORD

"There was an evening in what you said." —Nayyirah Waheed

I first met Jason Logan a few years ago, when a mutual friend, the writer Claudia Dey, introduced me to him in a sort of Henry James way, by sending me some examples of ink he had made in his kitchen out of torched peach stones, blackened Manila clam shells, and hand-harvested kerosene.

Being a writer who still uses ink to write out, and then cross out, each early draft of a manuscript, even into this twenty-first century, I had to meet him. We sat down in his kitchen and it felt like being introduced to someone with the skills of some lost medieval craft. What he did seemed a blend of alchemy with foraging and some possibly illegal art of cooking. Whenever we met, our conversations began over a delicious homemade soup, and then, on the very same table, he would begin to show me unknown inks of great subtlety and boundless colors that he had recently concocted and invented. Inks made out of lichen, wild grapes, rusty nails, drywall dust harvested from an overpass, and, most recently, an ink derived from gunpowder. Often in that small kitchen, while soups and these other ingredients were being heated up in saucepans to make those new inks, the border between food and ink tended to be porous. In fact, at one time he did say that he always felt I was a bit careful around his soups.

—Michael Ondaatje

INTRODUCTION

"Only a blinking eye can measure the light." —Sandra Beasley, "Inventory"

When I begin, it's not immediately promising. I've been up since early morning, it's a big gray city, and this is unfamiliar terrain. I get off way up at 157th Street at the edge of Washington Heights, without a clue what aboveground will look like. There's a man selling something out of a rolling suitcase, a couple of bodegas selling bedazzled cell phone cases and cigarettes, and a lone, vaguely Italian restaurant that lets me recharge my cell phone behind the bar after I buy a gritty espresso. The only other place to eat is McDonald's. And the sky looks like rain.

At the top of the hill is a little graveyard. It's fully fenced, forcing me to walk down the hill and through the wrought-iron gates to get back up to it. The sidewalks are rolling with acorns. Perfect little butterscotch-colored nuts with gentlemanly dark brown stripes up their sides. Only the caps are useful to me. I collect and shuck, filling a bag in just a few minutes. Inside the graveyard, it's empty. I search for lichen that feeds on the minerals of the old gravestones. There are beautiful examples of copper and bronze, too. Bleeding onto the stone is an almost fluorescing gray-green-blue—a color made by the same gradual chemical reactions that turned the Statue of Liberty green—a color made by time.

Out the gate and down the hill, the road ends in pipes, bolts, and heavy construction equipment. I walk past and through an old underpass. Everything smells like limestone. There is water dripping, graffiti, crystals growing—a kind of urban cave. I keep following it, using the flimsiest of maps, printed out from an email. My phone is about to die. The rain falls. Every crevice of the city is dripping but I am being pulled along this path. Rust pushing up from under layers of industrial paint. I collect some of these three-toned chips of color in a zip-top bag and label it. I walk along a bridge over the train tracks. Up high there are vines climbing the fence. More silver rain. Down metal stairs, cars rushing. I am under the Riverside Drive highway. Huge piles of construction aggregate. Red dirt. Yellow dirt. Rough gray pebbles. I take a sample of each. There is water gushing out of an old pipe like an industrial sculpture. Minerals and metals join beautiful oxidations of color all around. Water surrounds Manhattan and marbles through it. It wears away at concrete, and rock, and steel while nurturing the toughest of the weeds. This is one of those wild spaces where the human and the natural alchemize. It's also the most promising place to forage. The kind of color I can work with.

————

It started with a strange little bottle of brown ink. I discovered it in the five-story art supply store Pearl Paint, on Canal Street, when I was in my twenties, living in New York and trying to make it as an illustrator. The label on the oddly shaped bottle read, "black walnut ink." And when I got it home, I really liked the way it worked; it was a pale caramel-brown when mixed with water and used as a background wash, but it darkened to an almost mahogany-black when brushed on in layers. I filled my sketchbook and used up the bottle so quickly I went back to the shop to buy more. But the shelf was empty. I learned that the inkmaker had stopped making it. For years I searched for that bottle, finding the odd person here and there making small batches of walnut ink, but never that same one.

Seven years later in Toronto, after moving back to start a family, I was biking to work and noticed a beautiful old tree growing in the park that I passed through every day. When I realized that it was a black walnut tree, the memory of that original ink came back to me, and this time with urgency. Here was a nontoxic, tree-based art supply that I could safely use with my kids.

The thing was, it was only spring, which meant months of waiting as the nuts slowly developed into the green hulls that would ripen to their full size, only finally falling in late September. Here was my first lesson in ink—really, its first ingredient: patience. Two month later the best hulls were on the ground, intensifying their spicy scent and rich tannins. Fighting off squirrels, I filled up my backpack and took as many nuts as I could carry home with me, where I cooked them up into a rich brown ink. I think I might have boiled that first batch for two days straight in a big steel pot on my stove, and the result was darker and deeper and more complex than even that first New York bottle. I was hooked. I could make enough walnut ink to last a lifetime. I tweaked the recipe, learned to intensify the ink outside without my stove, learned about

shellac as a binder, and started designing labels for my black walnut ink.

But I wasn't done: As beautiful as brown can be, I couldn't help but begin to wonder about other colors, plants, and lost recipes. Because I began foraging in a city, it wasn't long before I started seeing color everywhere. Vines, roots, nuts, berries, and common weeds suddenly offered new possibilities. Alongside the greenery I collected from parks and back alleys, I started adding rusted nails, pieces of copper wire, and other industrial materials to my mostly plant-based search for handmade pigments.

———

Back in New York, foraging for color, I get the feeling of coming full circle. With my bike hidden in the weeds, I'm hopping fences, backpack full of vines, the tiny stars-on-skeletons of wild carrot, perfect porcelain berries (*Ampelopsis glandulosa*), each treasure snug inside a zip-top bag labeled with the location where it was found. It's getting dark and I have ventured deeper into Red Hook, Brooklyn. I am trying to harvest the rust from bedsprings, or more specifically, trying to wedge an X-shaped spring out of the frame and through the fence. I realize I've forgotten the key to the apartment I'm staying at. I'm trying to figure out where I am. My phone dies. I suddenly forget what people do when their phones die. This, after a beautiful ferry ride up the Hudson where I actually managed to forage paint off the boat floor. Cold and tired and in the growing dark, I see a place that sells key lime pies in the distance. The pie seller is an aging rockabilly, and when I ask if there is a library or something nearby where I could plug in a phone, he turns around and behind him is every cell phone charger imaginable. "Give me forty-five minutes," he says. So I buy one of his miniature pies. It is tart and sweet and perfect in its crumbly graham-cracker crust. I start to relax; I feel like I am on the right path. He asks what I am doing. I tell him about looking for wild grapes, and he says that the warehouse right next door houses an artist who makes big money crushing up flowers to make enormous paintings. Recharged, I walk next door to meet the artist's young assistant. I take some notes, and then walk farther down the block to find a little community garden where, finally, there is a tiny stand of dark purple wild grapes. I'm still thinking of the pie, which I can only compare to a perfect peaty scotch after having walked all day on a remote Scottish island in the rain—when the thing you didn't know you were looking for proves the most delicious.

Eventually I find my way down to the water. I am suddenly struck by the feeling that I am not alone. Hair prickles on the back of my neck. First, there is the unmistakable sound of wings. A huge hawk lands on the rough rocks at the river's edge. It turns just its head, its eyes emitting a weird, fearless energy. I understand why they say "the eyes of a hawk." They're like a magnet. Or Chernobyl. Something you can only respect with a shiver for its absolutely focused, cold beauty. We stare at each other for the longest time, as the bridge hovers dreamlike in the distance. After a long time, the hawk rises in the air and I see what it has in its talons—a huge long-tailed rat. I continue collecting the brackish Hudson River water. Everything I harvest today is in preparation for a *New York Times* Facebook Live drawing show. Foraging for color always leads me to engage with the most strange and remote parts of the city. My hands are freezing, I stop at McDonald's for a large order of hot, golden fries, and this is a perfect day.

––––––

I have been invited to the *Times* as the founder of the Toronto Ink Company, and my commission is to distill the colors of cities into ink. With my backpack full of pokeberry juice, old rocks, fungus, wild grapes, bits of mica, and acorn caps, I feel like a bit of a feral hippie among the tweed, starched white shirts, and graph paper of the *New York Times* building. I discover that some of the best inkmaking supplies I FedEx-ed ahead of me have broken and spilled en route. We have ten minutes to set up. I've had four coffees; Antonio, the host, took a shot of something. I don't have a second to think of what I'm doing— the cameras are rolling, and I begin to make ink.

At this moment, people from all over the world are viewing the *New York Times* Facebook page, where live video of my makeshift workspace is feeding out. These visitors ask me to draw what they are feeling right now: emotions ranging from joy to depression and everything in between. It's right before the 2016 US presidential election, and all eleven stories of the *New York Times* building are electrified. The drawings are a kind of abstract bouquet of color interactions. A shellac-based black ink cracks and separates into a pool of bright-pink pokeberry ink. Cloudy blobs of ash-gray and rusty orange commingle to suggest sadness and anger. Wild-grape purple and turmeric yellow blossom like joyful flowers. With each shout-out on Facebook I add a new drip of color or a splash of texture to the paper. I try to avoid getting my head in

front of the camera, as I consider each mood coming in through Facebook. I try to shape my makeshift palette of New York ink materials into something that feels beautiful, suggestive, and responsive to the audience. All my focus is on twelve inches of white watercolor paper. Two hours later, I look up. My hands are berry-stained, and powders and liquids and empty dropper bottles litter our little room in the New York Times building. Though I felt engrossed and alone as I completed each drawing, I am told that three hundred thousand people were watching me.

———

I am often asked what exactly ink is. It's not paint—which is a liquid color used mainly for creating images or covering surfaces. What distinguishes ink from other art supplies is its use as a tool for communication. People have been leaving marks with berries, burnt sticks, or colored rocks since the dawn of humanity—but the use of ink as a transmitter of *language* can be traced back to the first evidence of civilization in China and Mesopotamia: most often on shards of pottery, featuring markings that historians say were at first mostly accounting ledgers. But ink quickly became more than a decorator or calculator. . . . In fact, ink and pen were as vital to the growth of civilization as the wheel or the cultivation of wheat. Gaining the ability to permanently mark symbols on a flat surface meant that ideas could be saved, transported, and shared. Recipes, mathematical formulas, banking, poetry, music, diagrams, history, philosophy, and stories are inseparable from the history of ink.

The symbolic qualities of ink are necessarily backed up by its material qualities: In order to succeed as a conveyor of culture and ideas, ink needs to have certain features. It needs to be a liquid—an easily manipulated substance—so that it flows to a fine point, forming clean lines that dry permanently on paper. The ink needs to be intensely pigmented for maximum legibility and longevity. And finally, its various recipes must work for a whole range of writing utensils: dip pens, calligraphy brushes, printing presses, ballpoint pens, and felt-tipped markers.

So, how is ink made to have these qualities? The basic formula is actually quite simple: color + binder + water or oil = ink. Or, as *Collins Dictionary* puts it, "Ink is the colored liquid used for writing or printing." From this simple definition, ink can take, and has taken, many different paths. For me, this has meant culling my inkmaking techniques from a wide variety of sources across time and place, including medieval recipes for Bible ink; hand-stapled, lichen-dyeing booklets by British craft revivalists; Han dynasty–era recipes for pine-sap black, printed from Google books; and Russian chemists' YouTube experiments with copper crystals. Through research and intensive trial and error I've gradually been able to refine my process.

While recognizing the importance of historical inks, printing inks, and ballpoint and fountain pens, this book offers a method and set of tools to make your own water-based wild inks that are best used with a dip pen or brush, and demonstrates what those inks look like on paper. The book is divided into three parts: Find Ink, Make Ink, and Test Ink. Find Ink lays out a few ground rules for foraging for natural ingredients. Make Ink helps you to set up your kitchen and touches on a basic recipe that works for almost any ingredient, before diving into a more complex guide that is organized by color. Each color section includes a bit of cultural context, a more specific recipe, and some suggestions for advanced methods and other natural color opportunities within that color palette. And, finally, Test Ink offers inspiration for trying out handmade ink on paper. Here, I've included my own ink tests as well as a selection of ink tests from artists around the world who use foraged ink colors in a myriad of ways.

In my experience, inkmaking is easiest when you are patient and remain open to everything. Some of the most interesting effects of handmade inkmaking happen when the unexpected happens. Wherever it takes you, the ink you make yourself can only be your own color. Follow your instincts. There is no wrong path. Good luck!

1.

INK

FIND

ON FORAGING

One hot summer day a few years ago, I set off with a team of eight color-collecting ten-year-olds, each equipped only with a canvas bag and a decent supply of sunscreen. It was my son's birthday, and he'd asked for an inkmaking workshop. Otis, one of my son's best friends, is a creative redhead whose interests range from the creation of alphabets to Korean subway systems to crafting graphic novels from the periodic table of elements. While the other kids were foraging for the more expected sources of color, like rose petals stolen from our neighbors' gardens and ripe mulberries fallen from a nearby tree, Otis was looking at the ground: "Can we make ink out of these?" He had collected dozens of cigarette butts from the sidewalk on our way to the park. My answer, as always, was, "Yes! Let's try it." I have made ink from the flimsiest of ideas and the unlikeliest of materials. The cigarette butts, once cleaned, filtered, and harvested for their tobacco, became an almost golden-colored ink. I later combined it with rust and stinging nettle to create a most extraordinary two-toned ink, one that eventually made its way into the carry-on luggage of an artist who journeyed to the Arctic Circle on an icebreaker boat. Otis saw the potential for ink in less obvious places, but he also approached the craft without any awareness of its rules or limits, the sort of thinking that inevitably leads to beautifully unexpected results—my favorite kind. I try to embody that same spirit when I make ink.

"Let's just try it and see what happens." This attitude is so important. Not in a college-hipster potluck, "who cares what I put in this casserole?" way, but rather in a René Redzepi, "what will happen if I slowly bake this carrot for seven days, topping it with a dusting of woodruff flowers, sourced from the perimeter of the carrot patch?" kind of way that respects the ingredients and their sense of place. As you attempt the recipes I've included throughout this book, I hope you'll always follow your curiosity wherever it leads you.

———

What follows is a set of foundational tips that work with any inkmaking adventure. I encourage you to be creative and find your own process—it can be as complex or simple as you like. For example, I work with an artist in Berlin whose ink drawing consists of saving saucers with drips of tea or coffee on them and letting the spills coalesce into beautifully abstract golden blobs. Color is everywhere, and inky effects appear in the most surprising of places. Crushing some berries onto a plate and dipping a brush into the raw juice might be the most vibrant artwork you make all year.

Be Prepared

Mostly this is common sense. Dress for a few kinds of weather, and you won't be forced to return home if the weather changes. Consider your footwear, and you will feel free to really explore. Educate yourself on poison ivy and any other noxious plants, and you can fearlessly collect anything that piques your interest. Don't try to eat plants you don't know. Bring along gardening gloves. Watch out for glass, needles, and rusty nails. Approach the unknown with caution and curiosity. Don't harvest flowers from your neighbor's garden unless it's really late at night and you are drunk and in love.

Hard-Won Color Is Worth It

I once spent a day searching an ancient oak savanna for oak galls (those little nubs that produce tannin, which when combined with iron makes ancient oak gall ink). It was a beautiful day in High Park, with foresty smells of last year's leaves and acorns on the ground. I lay down and looked straight up at huge old trunks reaching fifty feet up; I felt like I was looking down instead of up, watching their branches feather out into space like roots against a brilliant blue sky. I returned home a bit depressed to have wasted a whole morning without a single surprising find. Later that afternoon I was walking my dog in the drizzling rain through the scrappy yard of the police station right across from our house when something caught my eye: a few new oak trees braced with rebar had been planted to replace last year's under-watered saplings. A bright green bulge was visible, where the scalloped edge of the oak leaf met the stem—an odd little globe of brighter green. An oak gall! It was an unforgettable lesson in just keeping my eyes open.

Color Is Everywhere

You don't need a huge national park to find natural color. Inkmaking supplies can be found anywhere plants grow. If you expand your palette to include industrial materials and ingredients from your own kitchen and grocery store, the possibilities become endless. For workshops I often lead a group along Toronto's railpath—a kind of industrial back alley reclaimed as a walking and biking path, following alongside a railway line that cuts a diagonal across the city toward the airport. Here detritus from condo developments meet native weeds, invasive shrubs, and wild grasses. I like to give each participant one square meter of random green space and have them look over their little patch carefully. The more you look, the more you see in what first appears as undifferentiated greenery. Dandelion and red clover compete with plantain, burdock, and vetch; below that, mosses and tiny sprouts that are hard to identify; below that, creeping vines of morning glory, seed husks from last year, black dirt, and the shell of a firecracker burnt out from some teenager's celebration. Just at the edge of the patch a few horsetail ferns are emerging, carrying with them the metals absorbed from the soil and the still-dormant but usable vines of wild grapes.

Color Might Come from Any Part of a Plant

My six-year-old daughter has learned to spot a bright purple blight, which tends to attack lamb's-quarter, a common sidewalk weed. What is this blight? We don't know, but we do know that when the afflicted leaves are crushed with vinegar, a brilliant magenta stains the water. If some part of a plant looks interesting to you, throw it in your sack. Bark provides tannins, the inner bark layer contains pigments, sap can act as a binder; leaves and new branches, buds, flowers, fruits, berries, lichen growing on an old log, roots, stems, nuts, and the hulls of nuts—these all carry intense colors. Pigmentation plays all kinds of different roles depending on type of plant, time of year, and even soil type. Pigments can act as a natural pesticide, a lure for pollinating insects, or a last gasp of color before dying (the evolutionary purpose of fall leaves' colors is still a mystery to scientists). Pigment is also key to photosynthesis (the green pigment chlorophyll attracts just the right wavelength of light to make energy) and can signal edibility or poison.

Do Your Research

I do two kinds of foraging. The first is picking a landscape and exploring it without preconceptions. In this version, I fill up my sack with all kinds of

different materials, taking note of where I find particularly promising specimens. I also take note (and samples) of the rocks, minerals, and human-made discoveries along my route. Wandering is research. The landscape can be as small as a patch of your own garden and as large as a field surrounding an abandoned reservoir, or the forest of a city park. Pay attention to the hardy weeds that grow in cracks, the vines that climb chain-link fences, and even the litter at your feet. Collecting is addictive. I also love the moment of returning home, when I spread out my finds across a table and sort and label all the possible avenues for future trips.

The second kind of foraging is more focused: the single-ingredient search. I like to pick one plant and try to find out everything I can about its traditional uses, habitat, and growing cycle. Very often the research starts with the plant's historical uses as a dye. If I know how its leaves were used in the past to color wool, I have an inkling of how I might make an ink out of it. Once I have chosen a plant to target and determined its natural habitat (for example: the buckthorn grows most plentifully at the brackish end of the park pond), it's mostly about watching and waiting until the plant is at its fullest and ripest. For some plants, the window for maximum color may be just one or two days. I then harvest as much as I can (so that I can try out a few different recipes with it), often calling on the help of children and friends. Berries can be juiced right away or frozen for later use. Nuts like black walnuts and acorns can be harvested and lose no color in being left to dry. Tougher plant matter like leaves, bark, or branches sometimes need to be fermented or left to soak in the backyard to break down and intensify.

A FORAGER'S CHECKLIST

- warm layered clothing and rain gear, where necessary
- weatherproof footwear
- a backpack or collecting bag
- zip-top plastic bags to separate finds
- permanent marker

- notebook and pen
- pruning saw
- pruning shears
- gardening trowel
- plant- or tree-finder reference book
- gardening gloves

ON FORAGING IN WINTER

Spring, with its special youthful quality, is an obvious time to forage; the year's first plants are verdant with chlorophyll, as each one emerges to compete for light and space. In later spring, as growth becomes more complex, you start to see how greenery works in layers and textures. The heat of summer multiplies the number of plants and flowers that can be collected; your eye is drawn to all the colorful possibilities. In fall, it is the spectacular changing of leaves and the ripening of berries and nuts that hold special significance to the color forager.

By winter, however, color seems to drain from the landscape. "Why forage in winter at all?" you may wonder. It turns out winter offers several unique advantages for the color forager. One is that the gray and white landscape of deep winter provides a dramatic and useful contrast for searching. You can see color where it appears from miles away. The wild rose hips, the last of the sumac fruits, or the fiery reds and oranges of the dogwood can all be collected. With less color overall to draw your attention, you'll also begin to notice textures and shapes that might prove useful to you. The bark of trees, galls of oaks, shells of nuts, and the curling vines of wild grapes all stand out in a muted landscape. If you know how to distinguish the skeletons of dormant plants, winter is a good time to see where plants will pop up in the spring. But most of all, without the greenery, winter is a time to forage for more industrial colors—especially materials that may be covered in weeds the rest of the year. In a city, this can mean bits of rust from iron or other useful metals like tin, copper, or aluminum. It can also mean bricks, masonry, flakes of white gypsum from drywall, spent firecrackers, and other waste that, while seemingly colorless, may provide a catalyst for a vibrant ink.

Still, winter foraging can be hard on the fingers and is never quite as productive as the rest of year. With less time spent outside, I find myself spending more time in the kitchen and studio, working with materials I've collected during the warmer months. This is the other secret advantage of inkmaking in winter, when the greatest discoveries often happen not at the level of root, leaf, and twig, but rather in glass beakers and old pots. Interactions between different inks, the rusting and oxidation of metals, the crystallization of salts and natural materials, and the fermentation of elixirs made the previous year—all thrive as the nights grow longer. Winter for me is a season of pure alchemy.

2.

INK

MAKE

WHAT IS INK AND HOW IS IT MADE?

Ink is color plus liquid. It can be created by breaking down color-rich base materials (called pigment, dyestuff, or tint) in a liquid (usually water), either by boiling or fermenting. Alternatively, the base materials can be ground into a powder and then mixed with a liquid.

Helpful Terms

Vehicle: the liquid in which the pigment is suspended. I use water most often, but the vehicle might be oil in the case of printing inks, gel in the case of block-printing, or alcohol in the case of marker inks.

Binder: a substance that acts as a kind of glue to bind liquid to color. Gum arabic is a very effective binder—I use it in almost every recipe.

Additive: This can include salt, vinegar, or metals that intensify the ink or make it more permanent, and thickeners that change an ink's consistency. You can also use a preservative like wintergreen oil, or a whole clove to keep the ink from molding—an important step for natural inks.

On Patience and Intensity

Boiling a bunch of flowers in a big pot of water will give you a kind of dye bath—a colorful liquid but not yet an ink. (What sets ink apart from dye is its intensity. While dye is immersive and meant to stain fabric evenly, ink comes in tiny bottles and is made for use on paper to make color-rich readable markings. That said, natural ink and natural dye are on friendly terms, often borrowing methods and folklore from one another.) When people come to see my inkmaking process they are sometimes disappointed to see that it is mostly just waiting and stirring and waiting some more. Unlike a recipe for cake, I can't give you a time and temperature for when your ink will be done. However, I can tell you how to achieve a condensed, intensified color. One way is to really grind your ingredients into their most smashed-up form. A second is to boil away a lot of the water, much like a reduction sauce in cooking. A third, slower method is to

let the water evaporate naturally by the sun, air, and time. The final way is to keep adding plant materials to your mix until you reach the desired vibrancy. A particularly tough plant might require a little bit of all of these methods. Once as much color as possible has been extracted from your material, you need to filter your ink down to its essence—although, even after filtering, I sometimes find myself boiling the ink down one last time. Natural ink is a whole landscape condensed into a little bottle. If the process seems slow and moves only a drip at a time, you are doing your job right.

The Kitchen Lab

I started an ink company in my family kitchen, and to a lesser extent in my third-floor attic. With the exception of the time I spent three days condensing more than one thousand cups of coffee into a sticky syrup (which made my whole house smell like old, burnt truck-stop coffee), my inkmaking hasn't been particularly disruptive. Since then I have set up a mobile ink factory in industrial hotel kitchens, in big working studios, in a park with a portable chef's stove on sawhorses, in friends' backyards, at campsites, and in the smallest studio apartment in the West Village. All you really need are some old pots (that you use only for inkmaking), a little space for working, some old utensils for stirring, a strainer, and a funnel. If you want to get more exact, it's fun to use lab glass, a cooking thermometer, litmus paper, a scale, and a mini beaker or two. A notebook chronicles your own recipes and experiments while adding to the citizen-scientist vibe. And this is not just show; inkmaking offers the chance to discover the way that color from the city works. How color changes and is held in suspension. How time and temperature affect a recipe, and how different seasons and different parts of a plant harvest different results. You are a scientist. Your kitchen is your lab.

NATURAL INK: A BASIC RECIPE

Here is my secret: Natural ink isn't that complicated. You can throw almost any pigment-rich base ingredient into an old pot with vinegar and salt, boil it up for an hour or two, add a couple drops of gum arabic, and voila—you have an ink. Think of ink as any colored water that's permanent on paper. All the recipes in this book will make 2 cups (480 ml) of ink, or about eight standard 2-ounce (60 ml) bottles. I've tried to be as exact as possible with quantities, but keep in mind that the final amount of ink you make will depend on how long you cook your ink and the how much liquid your foraged material might contain. Your goal should not be a set amount of ink but rather a color and consistency that feels right to you. If your ink is too thin, keep cooking; if your ink gets too thick, add a bit more water. Unlike a fine French sauce, it's pretty hard to "ruin" an ink. And sometimes a very faint ink, if collected from a very special plant, can become a favorite.

MATERIALS

Note: These are the materials I recommend every inkmaker have handy. You won't need every single one for every recipe, but the more tools you have available, the more techniques you can try.

water
a colorful base ingredient (such as berries, rocks, charcoal, nuts, roots, or leaves)
potato masher
measuring cups and spoons
mortar and pestle
a pot that you don't mind devoting to inkmaking
spoon or stir stick
white vinegar (cleaning grade if you can find it)
salt
thick white paper, for testing
gum arabic (a binder you can get at most art-supply stores)
wintergreen oil or whole cloves
glass containers with tight-fitting lids
sticker paper, for labels
glass muller or palette spatula, to be used on a glass surface
large bowl

fine-mesh strainer or colander
funnel
an old coffee grinder (optional)
coffee filters
funnelglass dropper
litmus papers
rubber gloves and some rags for cleanup

STERILIZING YOUR MATERIALS

Note: Sterilization is especially recommended for any recipe that requires plant-based materials.

1. Place clean bottles, dropper, caps, and utensils in a large saucepan.

2. Add enough water to cover all the equipment, making sure there are no air bubbles.

3. Bring the water to a boil, and boil rapidly for 5 minutes.

4. Turn off the stove and allow the water to cool completely.

METHOD

1. Prepare the Base Color Ingredient

For berries: Crush the berries using a potato masher. Add ½ cup (120 ml) water and 2 cups (450 g) berries. Then skip to step 3.

For rocks, charcoal, or other dry pigments: Grind ¼ cup of the material down to the finest dust using a mortar and pestle or similar. Add 2¾ cups (660 ml) water and 2 tablespoons gum arabic.

For nuts, roots, or leaves: Combine 2 cups (480 ml) water and 1 cup (120 ml) of plant material in the pot as is.

2. Intensify the Color

Put the base color ingredient into a large, old pot. Add 2 tablespoons vinegar and 1 tablespoon salt.

Heat to just below boiling and cook for at least 2 hours, stirring occasionally, until you have an intense ink color. (Dip a strip of paper into the colored water to test the intensity.) Remove from the heat and let cool.

3. Filter the Color

If you have large pieces of plant matter, like roots and leaves, first remove this material with a colander placed over a bowl, with the bowl catching the colored liquid. For a further level of filtering, place the small end of a funnel into the mouth of a glass container and fit a coffee filter into the funnel. Pour your strained liquid through the funnel slowly. The coffee filter should remove smaller particles, creating a cleaner ink. This step is particularly important if you plan to use the ink in a pen. To keep a pen writing smoothly, you need to use less binder, which can gum up the nib, and filter out any little grains of plant matter. On the other hand, for painters, some texture in the ink may be a positive—you can always refilter it if it seems too grainy.

4. Make It Permanent

Add gum arabic as a binder only after your ink is its desired color. For each 2-ounce (60 ml) bottle of ink I usually use 10 drops of gum arabic. If you're using a dry pigment as a base, you'll need to use more binder (usually 1 teaspoon per 2-ounce (60 ml) bottle). If you plan to use your ink for a pen, try to limit yourself to just a few drops of gum arabic for each small bottle. Add a few drops of wintergreen oil, or 1 whole clove, to each bottle to keep the ink from molding.

5. Bottle It

Any small glass jar or bottle with a tight-fitting lid can work for storing the ink. Your ink will last longer if you sterilize the bottle first with some boiling water. See instructions on page 48.

If you want to get fancy, you can find old empty ink bottles online or save small glass jars and bottles from your kitchen. You can also buy empty 1-ounce (30 ml) bottles in bulk. Label the ink with a sticker, give it a name, and list the ingredients, time, and location of the harvest. The labeling gives your ink meaning and also helps as a reference for later ink experiment comparisons.

6. Test It

A single drop of natural ink on paper will develop a lot of subtleties as it dries, often intensifying as it evaporates and darkening toward the edges. Another level of variation emerges as you test the ink using various tools: ink droppers, pens, nibs, brushes, and even sticks or feathers change the effect of the ink—as do different paper stocks.

7. Clean Up

While natural ink tends to stain less intensely than chemically produced ink, inkmaking can get messy and can stain clothes, countertops, and wooden spoons, so having rags, soap, and paper towels nearby can help keep you and the non-inkmaking members of your household on friendly terms.

FOR THE MORE ADVANCED INKMAKER

From the world of natural dyeing comes a whole range of potential additives (including mordants, which are used to help dye "bite" into a fabric). Additives like alum, copper, and iron oxides, and cream of tartar (found in the spice aisle), can help to shift the color, make your ink more permanent, and give it more intensity on paper. Other additives like baking soda, salt, vinegar, wine, borax, and lye can be used to change the color of a natural ink by modifying its pH (acidity and alkalinity) levels.

THICKENERS AND BINDERS

After color, consistency is the most defining feature of an ink. The easiest way
to thicken an ink is by cooking it until it reaches your desired texture, adding
more water as necessary to thin it back out. But nothing compares to the
texture created by agar, a seaweed-based ingredient (available at most health
food stores) that gives ink a gel-like texture perfect for use on textiles. A thicker
ink works well in block and silkscreen printing. Meanwhile, a shinier, more
layerable ink is great for brushwork, and the milk-based casein ink I make has
some amazing cracking effects.

Binders like shellac flakes or gum arabic will thicken ink, and also help
to fasten particles of color to the water that they are suspended in. A plant
with a strong dye effect like wild grape or black walnut doesn't always need a
binder, but for carbon- and soot-based inks, as well as rock- and mineral-based
inks, this binding effect keeps the particles of color from simply drifting to the
bottom of the ink bottle. The photograph on the opposite page depicts (clockwise from top left): liquid gum arabic, casein powder, shellac flakes, gum arabic
powder, and agar.

WATER

Despite what you may think, water isn't neutral. Its subtleties cannot be ignored by the inkmaker. For example, falling rainwater is naturally "soft," containing only sodium ions. As it makes its way through the ground, it picks up minerals like chalk, lime, salt, and magnesium. Soap bubbles up way better in soft water. Lye (a favorite medieval ingredient often used in sap green ink, page 124) is made when rainwater is run through the white ashes of hardwoods such as maple or oak. Water pulled from limestone rock will have a higher pH level, which will change the color of the ink. Seawater makes a different sort of ink altogether. For the exacting natural colorist, where you collect your water is as important as where you collect your plants and minerals.

GLASS

Consider for a moment the genius of glass. It's pure alchemy: When lightning hits a beach the extreme heat fuses sand into "thunderglass," a meeting of sky and ground that forms something clear as air but hard as rock. Color and light shine through clear glass. Glass is pH neutral and the standard for experimentation, mixing, and experiencing a glass of fine wine. I use glassware to mix inks, test out new formulations, and ferment ingredients, and I especially love the neutral, laboratory feel of a clear glass funnel. Start collecting tiny glass containers now. Each glass vessel gives a different feeling to the ink you make; add a clean white label and you'll have made a tiny bottled landscape.

PIGMENTS

Pigments are responsible for the reflection and absorption of different wavelengths of the rainbow of visible light. Almost every living thing has a color of some sort, expressed by what's called biological pigment. But just because a plant is brightly colored doesn't mean it will retain that same striking pigmentation when it is boiled down. Chlorophyll makes plants green, hemoglobin makes blood red, and melanin gives skin its darker tones; none of these natural pigments offer much to the inkmaker. On the other hand, pigments such as anthocyanin, which is common to purple foods, and curcumin, which is responsible for turmeric's yellow hue, are biological pigments that I've found to be quite effective.

Don't forget: Color for ink doesn't just come from plants; vivid color can be mined from several varieties of bugs (most famously kermes and cochineal insects), as well as from a range of rocks, minerals, and metals.

THE GROUND RULES
OF NATURAL INKMAKING

The laws of inkmaking, like ink itself, can, at times, prove quite elusive. Clear rules seem to bleed out of their solid lines the minute they are tested. But through my research, I have scratched out a few rules of thumb that have been useful to me.

Ink Is Alive
Stop worrying about how long your color will last in its current state and start delighting in the way it changes.

Learn with Your Hands
Fingers are an incredibly calibrated tool for understanding our environment. In a groundbreaking 2013 study, Swedish scientists at the KTH Royal Institute of Technology showed that people can detect nanoscale imperfections while running their fingers upon a smooth-as-glass surface. One researcher described this nano-sensitivity as the ability to distinguish between a house and a car, if you happened to have a fingertip the size of Earth. We really do learn by feeling things out! Stained hands are the reward and mark of a color pioneer.

Do Your Research
I like to start with a single ingredient and read as much as I can about it. More often than not the best information comes from recipes for natural-dyeing wool and other fabric. These tried-and-true recipes, which come from many different cultures around the world, tend to be more thorough than those for inkmaking.

Color Is a Moving Target
In her book *Color: A Natural History of the Palette*, Victoria Finlay notes that color is not something that a substance "has," but rather something that it "does." For example, buckthorn is capable of producing yellow, green, blue, purple, or magenta ink. Add a drop of lye to fresh buckthorn juice and you might see every single one of these colors come to life on the page. Similarly, I sometimes set out to make a certain color—say an intense black from acorns—and end up with a gradated silver-gray. For this reason, I like to save a few different versions of any given ink, and, as someone who produces small batches of wine might, I appreciate the variation from year to year in the same recipes.

Failures Can Be Beautiful
Beautiful because they're unexpected. Beautiful because they teach you something you didn't know about the materials. Beautiful because they lead you to the next thing. Beautiful because sometimes the thing you think you want is not the thing you really want.

Let the Ink Do Its Thing
Ink runs in rivulets that form their own rivulets; it begins with clear, clean lines and ends up bleeding, feathering, and staining. Natural ink is even more unpredictable. As much as possible, I try to get out of the way of the materials and appreciate the surprises that naturally result.

Record Your Experiments
While it's great to watch the ink you made evolve, change, and run amok, it's impossible to replicate and package up the brilliant mistakes you make unless you are recording as you go along. My personal archival method of choice is Instagram coupled with a German graph-paper notebook. Your homemade ink came from a place and time, a little corner of the world that is worth noting. So get yourself a notebook and keep records.

Go Weird
Is it okay to make ink from cigarette butts? Of course!

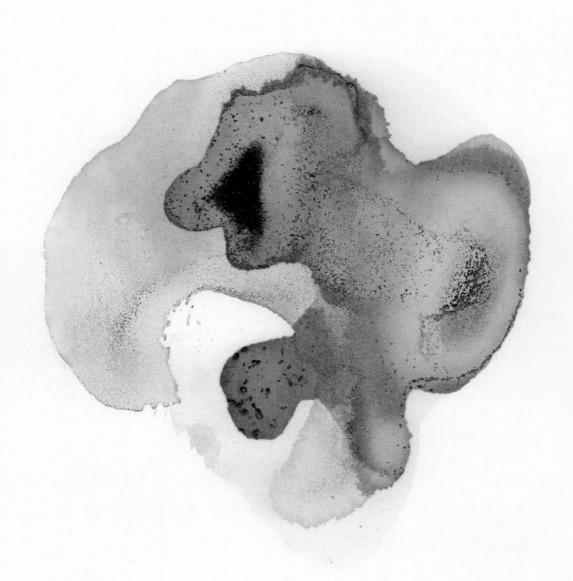

COLORS AND RECIPES

A NOTE ON COLOR

Today I got up early to prepare for an inkmaking workshop at a local art gallery. I am competing with two squirrels and a twitchy bird to harvest the little ripe black-purple berries of the mulberry tree a few streets down, in the richer part of my neighborhood. The streets are one-way and windy, and the homeowners scrub their Victorian bricks to a rich terracotta, buying pricey rocks and grasses that look pulled from northern ditches for their tiny front yards, yet they largely ignore their trees. Mulberries are alive with anthocyanin—the pigment that makes them purple—and I know I can make anything from gray to teal to purple ink with them. On my way home from the gallery, eyes to the ground, I notice the pink pattern on the green leaves of lamb's-quarter. I can't recall the name of the pest that produces the spray of magenta-purple spots, but I know that if mortar-and-pestled with vinegar and a bit of salt, the leaves will release a bright pink pigment that makes a beautiful, subtle ink. I am slowly teaching myself where to find the colors native to my neighborhood, and the amateur botany that I need to know regarding which plants to harvest and which to let alone. Yet the more I collect and experiment with color, the more mysterious it becomes.

Color doesn't live in material. It lives in light. Well, kind of.

Consider the last of the wizards, Sir Isaac Newton, and his *annus mirabilis*. In 1665, he was forced to leave Cambridge University when it closed as a precaution against the Great Plague. He spent the remainder of the year and all of 1666 at the home of his parents. Far from languishing in the countryside, however, Newton invented the precursor to calculus (with the way cooler name of *fluxions*), built his own metal forge (for alchemy—but that's another story), invented the world's most powerful telescope (by hand and using metal that he forged, of course), and began to consider gravity.

It was also in 1666 when he closed all the windows to his room and poked a tiny hole in his shutters. The tiny hole offered light a clean line into his room. He then positioned a toy prism in the beam and watched white light split into all the colors of the rainbow on his wall. The young Newton then placed a second prism in front of the rainbow on his wall and saw the colors channeled back into a single white beam. Besides being a why-didn't-I-think-of-that experiment, it also said something about color and light that is both simple and shocking. Light doesn't illuminate color. It *is* color.

The way we talk and think about color hasn't totally caught up with this revelation. Light is made up of all the colors, each one vibrating at a different frequency. So when we say an ink is blue, it's not that it contains blue, but rather it is giving us back blue light while absorbing all the other color vibrations. As mentioned previously, journalist Victoria Finlay wrote that we should think of things not as "being" a color but as "doing" a color. When you add electron-rich pinkish iron water to the warm brown tannic acid extracted from oak trees and see the water darken to an even, velvety black (see oak gall ink, page 84), then dry on your paper, it seems obvious: Ink is alive and busy. So is color. And before you ask—in the world of ink, the answer is yes: Black is a color.

I have divided this section up by color, recognizing that a single substance might make a whole range of colors, and that any single color can be made in a number of different ways. Therefore, the divisions are admittedly a bit arbitrary. Exactness doesn't really suit colors: black, red, yellow, purple, green, gray, orange, brown, and blue can't be satisfyingly explained by science. Our sense of color is historical, emotional, political, pop-cultural, and religious, and it goes back a long way before Newton. Color, the way I experience it, is a playground where science and magic meet. Have fun.

BUCKTHORN

POKE BERRY INK
(GLEN HIGHLANDS) 2017

HAWAIIAN TURMERIC
ALCOHOL INK 02/01/18

SAP GREEN
(NOV 2017)

CARBON BLACK
(GRAPE VINE) 01/18

BLACK WALNUT
(QUEENS PARK) 2017/18

WILD GRAPE PURPLE
(DUNDAS OVERPASS 2017)
COPPER OXIDE BLUE
ACORN CAP SILVER
SAFFLOWER
PINK 01 18
OAK GALL BLACK
GYPSUM WHITE

BLACK

"Black feeds in the depths of all color; it is their intimate abode."
—*Gaston Bachelard,* La Terre et les rêveries du repos

I once cooked a peach pit for seven hours in my oven. After a few hours, it started smoking. For the same project, I borrowed my friend Don's antique hurricane lamp and burned kerosene in it all night. Then I collected the slightly sticky soot for an ancient ink called lampblack. My project was based on the hints and suggestions of the poet Lorna Goodison, whose poem "To Make Various Sorts of Black" draws upon the almost unfollowable recipes of the most famous how-to writer of the Renaissance, Cennino Cennini. I learned from this poem that almost anything can be reduced to ashes, ground down to a fine powder, and made into an ink. In attempting to replicate these Renaissance recipes in my kitchen, I was learning something about the history of ink.

Carbon black is the oldest of inks. It has been found embedded in the earliest letterforms on clay, paper, papyrus, bone, and animal skin. Carbon black ink has been made from bone, grapevine, pinewood, olive oil, ivory, shells, and the stones of peaches; in truth, any dry, once-living material can be used—you just need a little fire.

I have a childlike love of the whole process of making black ink: First comes the chaos of fire, burning things down to ash; then you bind the soot to water; and then you guide it across paper, forming it into words. If the ash is improperly mixed, the result is a kind of pixilated haze—beautiful in its own right. The Chinese, who may have invented (and certainly perfected) carbon ink, demanded that the black pigment be ground down at least fifty thousand times in order to achieve a perfect black. They also added pearl dust, sculpting the mixture into elaborate, dry ink sticks, that could make ink as needed by being ground into an inkstone's small well of water. Early Chinese inkmakers are also credited with inventing India ink—a variation that combines shellac with the usual soot recipe, resulting in a waterproof shine.

When I make carbon black I like to picture the Bedouin shepherd who stumbled across a hole in the West Bank in 1947 and found himself in a cave containing possibly the origins of the Bible as we know it. These most sacred of texts were dubbed the Dead Sea Scrolls (which admittedly the brothers sold for the equivalent of about $30 at a local market). The desert conditions, sealed canisters, and hidden cave probably helped preserve this priceless cache, but the beautifully legible characters of two-thousand-year-old Hebrew calligraphy also owe their survival to the ink itself. Carbon ink (as long as it is not wiped away) will last forever without fading. Its rich, contrast-heavy black has transmitted most of what we know about the origins of writing and drawing. It was, after all, carbon ink—or at least charcoal scratching—that made the first human marks on cave walls at Chauvet in France, El Castillo in Spain, and the handprints on the Indonesian island of Sulawesi. Carbon-based ink was even used as a tattoo ink for Ötzi—the 5,300-year-old mummy found in 1991, in the Ötztal Alps between Austria and Italy—its patterns tracing out a record of his arthritis and broken bones and other injuries.

Part of what I love about carbon black is how many ways there are to achieve it. I am particularly fond of horsetail plants, which were also a favorite of the late Oliver Sacks. Horsetails or *Equisetum* have been thriving since dinosaur times; today they can often be found skirting railroad tracks. I like to make a horsetail-ash ink because I know that the plant pulls metals from the soil, which gives the ink a subtle metallic quality, but pretty much any dried organic material can be reduced to ashes, ground up, and made into a good black ink. Below is the recipe for vine black ink, a recipe that was popular with Renaissance calligraphers and (if you don't mind repetitive tasks) is relatively easy to make.

VINE BLACK INK

COLLECTION

Grapevines are the classic material for making vine black. In Toronto's Little Portugal, where I live, grapevines appear on the sidewalks, bundled with twine, in late fall and early spring, when home wine-makers clear out last year's garden waste. If you know someone who makes wine, they will be happily surprised by your request. Wild grapevines are pretty common in most cities, growing along fences and up trees in almost any green space. Thicker parts of the vine have a distinctive shaggy texture. Cut off 6-inch (15-cm) lengths of vine about the width of your baby finger with pruning shears. Twenty or so pieces of vine will make a good-size batch of ashes. If you can't find grapevine, any dried woody vine will work—or even small sticks (birch, willow, and alder buckthorn are particularly good). If you don't want to collect your own vines, most art supply stores sell vine charcoal, which can be ground down to a fine dust. Still too difficult? Kremer Pigments sells vine charcoal as a finely ground pigment.

MATERIALS

20 6-inch (15 cm) lengths grapevine, burnt to ash,
    or ¼ cup (24 g) charcoal powder
mortar and pestle
1¾ cup (420 ml) water
3 tablespoons gum arabic
large bowl
glass container with a tight-fitting lid

METHOD

1. If using grapevine, grind down the carbonized grapevines with a mortar and pestle until you have an extremely fine powder (see How to Make Vine Charcoal for Ink or Drawing on page 80). If using store-bought charcoal powder, proceed to step 2.

2. In a large bowl, gradually combine ash (or charcoal powder) with water and gum arabic, a tablespoon of each ingredient at a time. This should give you a syrupy black liquid. Use the pestle to stir and grind this liquid until silky.

3. Slowly add more water (about 3 to 4 tablespoons, 45 to 60 ml) until the mixture is the consistency of ink.

4. Pour into the glass container. To further integrate water, binder, and pigment, cover tightly and shake the container of ink vigorously.

Use: Test out your ink on paper. If the color is not black enough, put the ink back in the mortar and add more carbon dust. If the ink appears grainy, you may need to grind the pigment down to finer particles, or else do some more stirring and shaking. If kept tightly capped, this ink should last forever.

Suggested color pairings: Over years of testing out inks, I've found certain inks work happily together on paper, but of course let your own instincts guide you. For vine black ink, I recommend pairing with wild grape ink (page 106) and/or silvery acorn cap ink (page 114).

Other sources of black: Vines, willow, and other wood burned to charcoal; peach pits; chimney soot; shells; and even pollution (there is a company called Air-Ink that is capturing car exhaust in Mumbai and making it into a rich black ink).

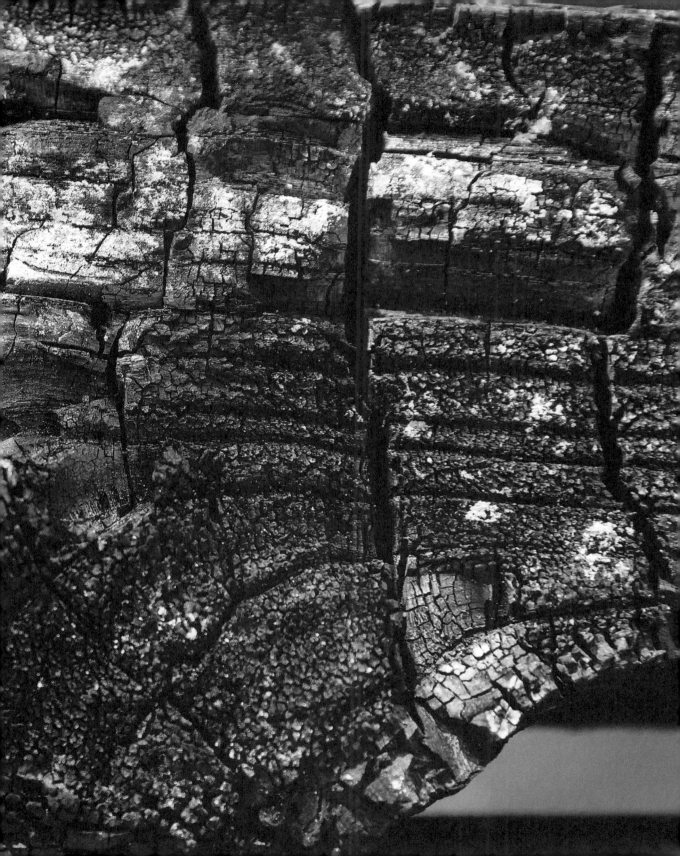

HOW TO MAKE VINE CHARCOAL
FOR INK OR DRAWING

Soft vine charcoal is easily found wherever you buy art supplies but is way cheaper and more satisfying to make yourself. Wood becomes charcoal when, without oxygen, the flammable gases and water in the wood are expelled and consumed by heat. The perfect tool for this process is the metal tin that Altoid mints come in; the tight but imperfectly sealing lid allows gases and steam to escape while protecting the wood from burning up.

TOOLS

Pruning shears
Vines or willow twigs
Empty Altoids tin, or other tin with a lid
Fire—a woodstove, small campfire, or barbecue
    grill can all work
Tongs
Mortar and pestle, or clean coffee grinder

METHOD

1. Use pruning shears to clip off lengths of vines or willow twigs.

2. Peel away any loose bark with your fingers and cut the lengths into roughly crayon-sized pieces.

3. Place a dozen or so of the pieces inside an Altoids tin or other metal container with a lid.

4. Build your fire. With tongs, place your tin at the center of the blaze. Let the tin sit in the flame for 1 hour.

5. With tongs, carefully remove the tin from the flame and set aside until cool to the touch, about 1 hour. Open the tin: each stick should be perfectly black and reduced in size by about a third.

6. Use a mortar and pestle or old coffee grinder to grind the charcoal sticks into powder. This will form the fine sparkly black pigments necessary for carbon black ink. Your charcoal powder can be stored in a clean Altoids container and used as a soft, erasable art material.

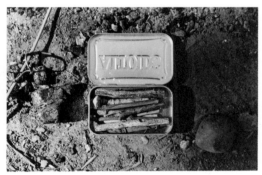

BLACKER

"If I could find anything blacker than black, I'd use it." —J. M. W. Turner

As dark and permanent and elemental as carbon black is, it's not a perfect ink: It's rarely waterproof and is easily wiped away. The solution to this is found (believe it or not) flying through the air on papery wings. The gall wasp lays her eggs in the new shoots of the oak tree, which reacts to the invasion by creating a hard lump in its bark; this odd little sphere, the oak gall, becomes the protective home of the wasp's babies. The interaction of larva and tree intensifies the oak tannins, the key ingredient for an ink that has defined two thousand years of written history. According to obscure medieval recipes I found on the internet, oak galls were crushed into wine and mixed with some sort of tree gum. But it is when ferrous sulfate (also called iron [II] sulfate) is added to the recipe that the real magic happens. Whether by alchemy, pre-chemistry, or luck, the formula creates a reaction between iron electrons, oxygen, and tannic acids to form a stable black ink, which, rather than sitting on the surface, is able to burn into and fuse with paper or vellum (parchment made of animal skin). The result is an inerasable ink called iron gall, oak gall, or, more recently, registrar's ink. It was the ink of record for weddings, funerals, and contracts; before that it was the ink found in one of the oldest surviving Bibles, the Magna Carta, and *Beowulf.* It was the favored ink of da Vinci, Victor Hugo, Bach, and the US Postal Service. This is an ink with pedigree. It's also pretty simple to make if you can get ahold of the ingredients.

OAK GALL INK

COLLECTION

It is said that the best oak galls come from Aleppo, but I have found them growing on the smaller twigs of oak saplings planted in front of the police station across from my house. Each oak gall is about the size of a gumball and green in the spring. Galls can appear on the stems or undersides of oak leaves. As they dry, they will become light brown, with a little hole visible where the wasp babies exited their first home. You can also order oak galls from specialty stores online (and don't feel bad—they really are hard to find in the wild). The other key ingredient, ferrous sulfate (known to medievalists more poetically as green vitriol or copperas) is made by bathing iron in sulfuric acid and collecting the resulting green crystals. Bottles of it are available wherever dye supplies are sold. You might also forage for it by purchasing iron supplements at your local drugstore.

MATERIALS

2 ounces (55 g) oak galls, completely dried and hardened
mortar and pestle or clean coffee grinder
large, old pot
coffee filter or fine cheesecloth
glass container with a tight-fitting lid
1 ounce (30 ml) ferrous sulfate, also called iron (II) sulfate (if you are using the supplements, they will need to be ground up to a fine dust)
gum arabic

METHOD

1. Crush the dried oak galls to a fine powder with a mortar and pestle or clean coffee grinder. Place the powder in a large, old pot.

2. Pour 2 cups (480 ml) water onto the oak gall material. Soak for at least a day.

3. You now have a solution of gallic and tannic acid. Strain the solution through a coffee filter or fine cheesecloth into the glass container.

4. Add the ferrous sulfate to the jar of gallic acid solution. Mix well.

5. Add a few drops of gum arabic to the solution.

6. Place a lid on the ink container.

Use: The oak gall ink will darken on the page as it interacts with oxygen. It does, over time, eat away at plant-based paper, so vellum is a more durable choice. This is the sort of ink you might consider using for medieval reenactments and treasure maps.

Suggested color pairings: Try with sap green ink (page 124) to keep within a medieval color scheme. But really, oak gall black goes with anything.

BROWN

"God has a brown voice,
as soft and full as beer."
—Anne Sexton, *"For Eleanor Boylan Talking with God"*

In 2009, British geologists made a fascinating find: a mysterious, cloudy ink, not quite black and not quite brown, dating back to before there was paper, quills, or even people. This prehistoric ink was discovered in the fossilized remains of *Belemnotheutis antiquus*, a squid-like creature that lived more than 150 million years ago. Embedded in the limestone fossil was the still-soft tissue of a perfectly preserved ink sac. The ancient brownish-black ink therein—its pigment a kind of melanin called *eumelanin*—was found to share the same makeup and purpose as the ink made by the modern-day octopus, squid, and cuttlefish. It also (with a little moistening) became the world's oldest functional ink when Dutch artist Esther van Hulsen used it to depict the creature itself, a work which can be seen at the Natural History Museum at Oslo. It was not the first time cephalopod ink was used by man, however. Cuttlefish ink was used intermittently in the ancient Greek and Roman worlds to write and draw; Leonardo da Vinci used it as both the ink and wash for many of his drawings. Today, this brownish-black color is commonly known as *sepia*, and is heavily associated with its use in early black-and-white photography.

Squid or cuttlefish ink is a bit tricky (read: odiferous) to work with, and hard to argue for, given that there's another more convenient source for rich dark-brown ink: black walnut. Here is an ink that comes ready to use from the green lime-like hull of the black walnut—a familiar urban tree with a distinctive leaf and delicious scent.

BLACK WALNUT INK

COLLECTION

Black walnut hulls are at their most pigment-rich by the end of autumn, when they are large (about the size of Ping-Pong balls) and very ripe. They can be plucked from low branches or harvested from the ground. Fear not rotting hulls—these make great ink. If you don't want to stain your hands, wear gloves as you cut or peel the green hulls from the hard nuts inside, dropping the hulls into a pot of water. The nut (in its shell) can be roasted in the oven and then cracked open between two cast-iron pans, revealing the small but peculiarly delicious nutmeat inside.

To get a layered, almost oil-paint like effect, I like to add shellac flakes (available at fine wood-working supply stores and the internet), which can be broken down in a solution of water and borax to form a shiny, syrupy binding agent. Shellac can get fussy, clumping up as it cools, and is really only recommended for the most patient of inkmakers.

MATERIALS

large, old pot
2 cups (300 g), or around a dozen, black
    walnut hulls
strainer
coffee filter
glass funnel
glass container with a tight-fitting lid
small glass bottles
wintergreen oil or whole cloves
2 tablespoons borax (optional)
¾ cup (180 ml) very hot water (optional)
spoon or stir stick (optional)
¼ cup (55 g) shellac flakes (optional)

METHOD

1. In a large pot, combine the walnut hulls with 2 cups (480 ml) water.

2. Heat to boiling and let boil for 3 to 4 hours, until you have a very rich, mahogany-brown color and the liquid has reduced by about one-third. Remove from the heat and let cool.

Note: If you have time, instead of boiling, try leaving the walnut hulls in water and out in the sun for a few days, or even a week. This saves energy and may even add new subtleties to the color.

3. Filter your ink first through a strainer, and then through a coffee filter–lined funnel emptying into a glass container.

4. Pour this filtered ink into smaller glass bottles for individual use.

5. Black walnut attracts mold, so after bottling be sure to add a fungicide such as wintergreen oil (a few drops) or 1 whole clove per bottle. If eventually you do find a layer of mold on top of your ink, simply remove it before using the ink.

BLACK WALNUT INK additional steps continue on next spread

ADDITIONAL STEPS (OPTIONAL)

6. Dissolve the borax in the hot water. Stir with a spoon or stick until completely dissolved.

7. Add the shellac flakes to the water very slowly, stirring constantly, until you have a yellowish, syrupy liquid.

8. Add 3 tablespoons of this shellac mixture to every cup of the finished black walnut ink or until the ink has a nice shimmer to it.

Use: Brown looks great with more brown. Try layering your ink until you get an almost black color.

Suggested color pairings: Brown lives happily with anything pink. Try safflower pink ink (page 128) in small amounts as a complement to brown.

Other sources of brown: Here is my list of favorite brown-yielding ingredients, although there are frankly a great number of barks, nuts, leaves, and roots that can offer a whole range of browns: plantain roots; coffee (espresso is great); fir, willow, or oak bark; tea; squid ink; dandelion roots; roasted chicory roots; phlox; butternut; and alder cones.

RED

"Red, I said. Sudden, red." —Robert Hass, "The Problem of Describing Color"

Red feels urgent, emphatic; the color of blood, love, and anger. The use of red ink to give emphasis, or to denote importance, or even to color words attributed to gods and kings, dates back to ancient times; it can be found in the Egyptian *Book of the Dead*, Imperial China, and Roman and papal edicts. The oldest reds are found in the earth itself in the form of iron oxides and ochres. Archaeological finds that include ground red rocks are used as evidence of human symbolic activity—which could mean body painting, cave painting, or other ways of using color to make meaning. Iron-based red has been used for war paint and cave paintings, and was thrown into rivers by artist Andy Goldsworthy. Making ink from iron mineral pigments or from pure rust feels primal and almost sacred in a way that's hard to put into words. Plus, iron ink really lasts. However, these inks tend toward the brownish/orange-ish tones of red, so when I was first experimenting with red, and looking for something more crimson, these options fell short. For a while sumac ink interested me, as its berries are a deep, rich red and its stems and leaves contain useful tannins. But again, the results were less jewel-toned and more earthy brown. So how exactly does one make bright red ink?

The answer was perfected by wandering Civil War soldiers. Deep in the New England woods grows the pokeberry bush (*Phytolacca americana*), with its perfectly globular berries arranged like fireworks on the forest floor. It is likely that pokeberry ink was used by the indigenous peoples of early North America (research indicates the pokeberry served a medicinal purpose for native tribes in Virginia and Delaware), by early settlers, and in feather quill pens by Civil War soldiers writing home to their loved ones.

POKEBERRY INK

COLLECTION

The pokeberry shrub grows to be six feet tall or so, with oblong leaves. These shrubs are most notable for their bright magenta stems with green, then white, then dark purple berries that hang in clusters like grapes. They grow in pastures, recently cleared areas, woodland openings, and along fencerows.

MATERIALS

large, old pot
4 cups (400 g) pokeberries
potato masher
fine-mesh strainer
large bowl
coffee filter
one clove per jar of ink
glass container with a tight-fitting lid

METHOD

1. In a large, old pot, crush and strain the berries with a potato masher, then filter everything through a fine-mesh strainer with a bowl underneath to collect the liquid. Discard any solids. A further round of filtering the liquid through a coffee filter should give you an ink that is free-flowing enough to use in a pen.

2. Add the whole cloves.

3. Pour the ink in a glass container with a tight-fitting lid. In a refrigerator, this ink can keep for up to a year. But make sure you label it carefully if you do keep it in your fridge.

Use: Pokeberry is the brightest of all the natural inks, although it will fade in the sun. Artwork made with pokeberry ink should be sprayed with a fixative (casein is a great natural option, or there are any number of art supply store selections) to protect the color, or you could simply accept it as a living, changing ink.

Suggested color pairings: Pokeberry ink goes beautifully with sap green ink (page 124), copper oxide ink (page 98), or silvery acorn cap ink (page 114).

Other sources of red: Rust, sumac berries, rose hips, kermes insects, cochineal insects, lichen, beets, raspberry, hibiscus flowers, and cherry juice.

Important Safety Note: All parts of the pokeberry plant (roots, stems, leaves, and berries) are poisonous if ingested. Use caution when handling the plant materials and finished ink; keep both out of reach of children and pets. Be sure to clearly label your ink and discard any plant materials with the utmost caution.

BLUE

"Blue is the color of longing for the distances you never arrive in, for the blue world."
—*Rebecca Solnit,* A Field Guide to Getting Lost

Oh, blue. It is the most open-ended of colors. Heaven, sadness, the ocean and sky, Frank Sinatra's eyes, the paintings of Picasso's Blue Period (1901–1904). In the world of ink, it dominates the ballpoint pen market, was once important for detecting counterfeit signatures, and pairs nicely with delicate powder-blue airmail paper. With just the right pH balance, it is possible to make a stable blue color from wild blueberries or grapes. The indigo plant also makes the beautiful blue still used to dye overpriced Japanese denim—but because it's not native to Canada, and because the recipe is really stinky, I have not spent much time with this natural pigment.

There is a color called *maljo* ("evil eye") blue: an intense purple-blue worn by those who wield *maljo* magic in Trinidad and Tobago. When I imagine a *maljo*-colored ink, I picture it to be iridescent like oil on pavement, a dark, intense blue that is almost black. I hope one day to travel to the Caribbean with my poet friend and learn to bottle such an ink. Until then, here is a magic (and slightly toxic) blue that is as old as ancient Egypt. This is the ink that changes color most over time. When oxygen and the mild acids in salt and vinegar meet a bit of copper wire or copper wool, a beautiful color emerges from the crystallizing chemical reaction that makes copper oxide. This is copper's version of rust.

COPPER OXIDE INK

COLLECTION

Copper can be found almost anywhere in a city. Pennies, copper wire, copper wool, or copper wire sponges (available from most hardware stores) are all great sources. I sometimes buy "copper chop," an industrial recycling product found deep in suburban industrial parks (check your local yellow pages).

MATERIALS

glass jar
½ cup (600 g) copper scraps
2 cups (480 ml) white vinegar, plus more
    as needed
1 tablespoon salt
spoon or stir stick
strainer
glass containers with tight-fitting lids
rubber gloves

METHOD

1. In a large glass jar, cover the copper with vinegar until fully submerged. Add the salt.

2. Leave the mixture in a well-ventilated area, uncovered, away from pets and kids, for 1 to 3 weeks, until you have a rich, blue-colored liquid. Stir twice a day, adding more vinegar as needed as the liquid evaporates to keep the copper pieces fully covered.

3. Once the desired hue has been reached, strain the ink and pour into individual glass containers with tight-fitting lids. The color may separate into a transparent, darker blue and a lighter, milkier liquid. Shaken together, these will form a beautiful drawing ink.

Use: Salt acts as a catalyst for the oxidation of copper. It also causes copper ink to form crystals on paper. This is an ink that will destroy a metal pen nib, but that looks beautiful brushed onto paper, with many variations and textures. The fun here is in experimentation.

Suggested color pairings: I love the turquoise blue of copper oxide ink with a glossy black India ink. It also pairs well with wild grape ink (page 106) or a light wash of black walnut ink (page 88–90).

Other sources of blue: The most intense source of natural blue is indigo, which makes a beautiful ink if you can find it. Cornflowers, black beans, woad, mulberries, blueberries, or wild grape juice with baking soda added to it are less permanent and less intense, but easier to deal with.

Important Safety Note: Use rubber gloves while following this recipe and work in a well-ventilated area. Keep both ink-in-progress and finished ink out of reach of children and pets.

PURPLE

"I think it pisses God off if you walk by the color purple in a field somewhere and don't notice it." —Alice Walker, The Color Purple

At a sort of secret favorite spot between the overpass and the train tracks near my house, there's a bit of scrubby green space thick with tree-size weeds, abandoned chunks of cement, and tattered plastic bags. It's a place I might never have noticed, if weren't for its abundance of wild grapes. The vines climb over the bridge railing and the fruit falls onto the sidewalk, leaving noticeable stains. The best grapes hang in high clusters from the tree branches halfway down the embankment. These are the small, almost black-purple fox grapes that can be crushed to make the most intense purple ink. I was told that the color from grapes is fugitive—that it fades and changes with time and light. But not these grapes—I have ink samples from years ago that still vibrate with color. The ink is great, but bear with me here because its color has a fascinating history.

Color associations vary across time and culture. Some cultures consider white the color of death; others say black. The color green symbolizes anything from the environment to jealousy to sickness to rebirth. Blue can symbolize depression, heaven, intelligence, and loyalty, to name a few. But purple, almost everywhere, and in almost every time period, is regal; a color of power, luxury, and ambition. Believe it or not, there is a pretty fascinating explanation for the origins of these virtually universal associations.

Deep in the eastern part of the Mediterranean Sea is the hunting ground of a spiky carnivorous creature of the genus *Murex*. Murex snails sedate their prey with a brownish liquid that when exposed to oxygen turns a distinctive shade of purple. This color, already rare in nature, was utterly singular as a colorant. Nothing could dye cloth like Tyrian purple (named for the Lebanese city of Tyre), and rather than fading, the color intensified over time. It was complex, expensive, environmentally destructive, and demanded a lot of slave labor. According to medieval historian David Jacoby, "twelve thousand snails of *Murex brandaris* yield[ed] no more than 1.4 g of pure dye, enough to color only the trim of a single garment." At the height of the colorant's popularity it was literally worth its weight in gold. The Phoenicians (whose name actually derives from a word for purple) were famous sellers and exporters of the pigment to Carthage, where it was adopted by the Romans as a symbol of imperial authority and status. And that's when purple got political.

Beginning with the reign of Alexander Severus (222–235 CE), only the emperor (or hand-picked VIPs) could wear purple silk outfits. Nero made even selling purple dye punishable by death. Purple ink was reserved for the decrees and seals of kings, emperors, and the pope. Recipes were closely guarded secrets. Whether due to overfishing or to war, it was somewhere around the Fall of Constantinople that the murex dyeing technique went into decline.

The hunt was on for a new source of rich, permanent purple. The European West turned to whortleberry or woad, two common European plants, over-dyed with madder (later used to color the redcoat uniforms of the British army). A slightly more intense purple-red came from the vermilion produced from the Kermes oak insect *Kermes vermilio*. Later, vermilion was replaced by carmine red, which is derived from the dried bodies of the female cochineal—a very small yet very significant bug that feeds on prickly pear cactus fruits. When Spaniards first came to Mexico, cochineal was one of their most valuable finds in the New World and became a Spanish state secret. Competing with cochineal for the superlative of weirdest red-producing method were two lichens, *Ochrolechia* and *Umbilicaria*, which grow on old rocks, gray and unassuming, but which turn bright purple and red when they react with ammonia, such as that found in stale urine. This valuable substance (now maybe purposefully forgotten) was for a moment the most important export of Newcastle upon Tyne, where it was harvested with contributions from those who were thought to produce the purist ammonia: prepubescent boys.

The story of purple has a few other twists and turns, but color historians seem to agree that the search for the perfect royal purple ended with the first chemistry-made dye pigment in 1856. The young chemistry virtuoso Sir William Henry Perkin, who at eighteen was an assistant at the Royal College of Chemistry, was assigned the project of trying to make a synthetic quinine for the treatment of malaria. On his Easter vacation, in a makeshift lab in his parents' house in East End London, he ended up accidentally discovering a brilliant purple color, secretly developing it further with his friend to create the first aniline dye, which he named *mauveine*. The dye was made primarily using chemicals Perkin had extracted from coal tar—an entirely abundant industrial byproduct in Dickensian England. Thanks to the tastes of British royalty, purple-colored dresses, particularly with hooped skirts, were just becoming popular; it seems everything kind of came together to make Perkin a very rich man, as he finally brought the desperate search for nature's perfect purple to an end.

It is hard to imagine a world in which each new color discovery was a new luxury, a world in which artists had to get their patrons to agree on color costs before beginning a commission. Perkin's success marked a beginning of the end for the natural color industry. The discovery and marketing of mauveine—more than any other color—would usher in an age of synthetic color production and manufacturing, an age that we are still living in. A world where every color of paint, dye, or ink is available to the consumer with predictable results and trademarked industrial sources. The early aniline dye-works corporations have become some of the biggest chemical producers of our era, including BASF, IG Farben, and Bayer.

All of this is to say that despite (or almost because of) the ability of chemistry to produce every conceivable color between blue and red, there is something deeply satisfying and powerful about discovering a natural, uniquely resilient purple pigment in a secret place near the railway tracks that only I know about—especially in this day and age. I still haven't figured out why the pigment doesn't fade the way so many other cyanin-based colors like cherries, beets, elderberries, and blueberries do. Maybe it has to do with fermentation, with the fact that the color of a wine often deepens over time. Perhaps some tinkering scientists will reveal the truth someday.

WILD GRAPE INK

COLLECTION

There are a handful of species of wild grape in North America, the most common being the fox grape. They are smaller than cultivated grapes, tend to be sour, and often grow high in trees. The vine is recognizable by its rough bark. Make sure you have a close look at photographs of fox grapes before foraging, as there are similar berries that are poisonous and not good for ink. They grow in abundance in hedgerows, roadsides, and untended lots—even in cities. They occur in every part of the world, excluding Antarctica. In the late fall, when they are most plentiful, a stand of wild grapes may be indicated by birdsong.

MATERIALS

large, old pot
4 cups (600 g) wild grapes (see Note; I like to collect a big potful when they are at their juiciest from mid to late fall)
potato masher
fine-mesh strainer
large bowl
coffee filter
wintergreen oil or whole cloves
glass container with a tight-fitting lid

Note: Some people find that the juice of grapes irritates their skin, and after an hour of picking, your hands will definitely be stained purple, so if either of these things worries you, be sure to wear gloves.

METHOD

1. In a large, old pot, combine the grapes with ½ cup (120 ml) water. Heat to just below boiling. Cook for 10 minutes, or until the liquid begins to thicken, occasionally crushing the grapes with a potato masher.

2. Pour the cooked grapes and juice through a fine-mesh strainer with a bowl underneath to collect the liquid. Discard any solids. A further round of filtering the liquid through a coffee filter should give you an ink that is quite easy to use.

3. Add a few drops of wintergreen oil or a whole clove to prevent molding. Pour the ink into a glass container with a tight-fitting lid.

4. Keep refrigerated.

Use: Wild grape, without any additives, makes a rich purple ink. You can control the thickness of the ink by how much water you add, as well as by how much is evaporated away as it's cooking. Because of the sugars in wild grape juice ink, you will want to keep all of your bottles sterilized (see Sterilizing Your Materials, page 48) and well-sealed, and store the ink in the refrigerator to keep it from fermenting.

Suggested color pairings: Wild grape looks beautiful with everything. I particularly like it with silvery acorn cap ink (page 114).

Other sources of purple: Lichen, purple cabbage, mulberries, blueberries, black beans, and red onion skins.

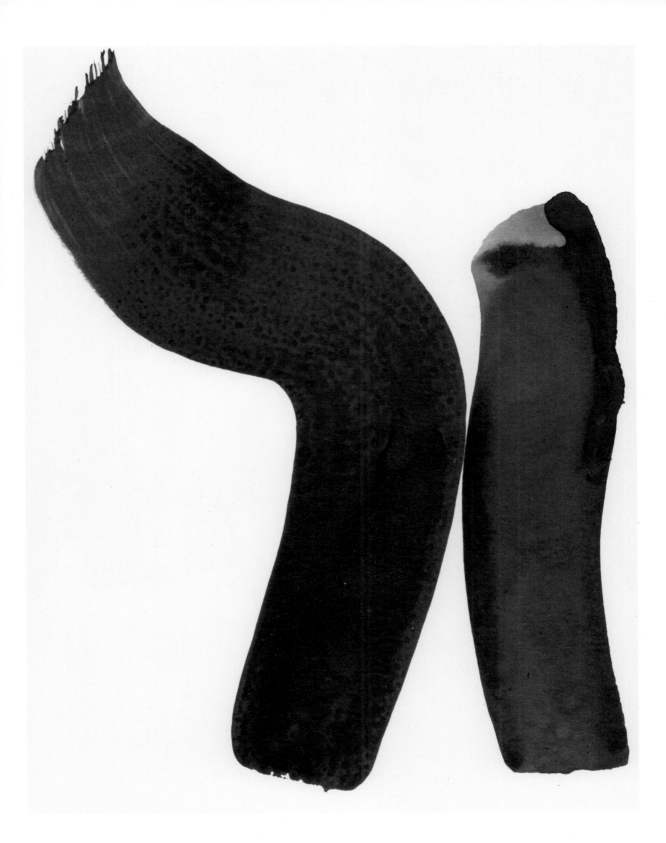

YELLOW

"The yellow glistens.
It glistens with various yellows,
Citrons, oranges and greens
Flowering over the skin."
—Wallace Stevens, *"Study of Two Pears"*

My ex-stepmother, whom I call Tutu-Lisa, is a tree farmer in Hawaii. It was on her land that I learned how to peel cinnamon and how to crack macadamia nuts. While there I read a bit about bird feathers as coloring for traditional Hawaiian costumes. She often sends me organic turmeric roots she grows herself; I have been grating and boiling them into ink for the past few years. Sometimes I substitute turmeric powder for the raw roots. While neither are strictly speaking city-foraged, the yellow from turmeric has become a staple color of the Toronto Ink Company. A couple of months ago I was reading up on turmeric and realized that the color is way more soluble in alcohol than it is in water. This inspired me to give marker-making a try, as marker ink is alcohol based, and I've always wanted to make my own markers. I like to use 98-percent rubbing alcohol from the drugstore, but if you can get ahold of a very high-proof ethanol alcohol like Everclear, or even some kind of intense homemade vodka, that would work just as well. Here, as usual, you will need a glass jar with a tight-fitting lid—this ink can really make a mess. The pigments in turmeric tend to fade over time. In India, where turmeric is plentiful and its color is highly valued, traditional dyers recognize that this is a living yellow color and will simply re-dye clothes that are beginning to fade with more turmeric. If your ink starts to fade, why not just add another layer?

TURMERIC ALCOHOL INK

MATERIALS

3 tablespoon turmeric powder, or 2–3-inch
    (5–7.5-cm) roots, peeled and grated
1¾ cup (400 ml) isopropyl alcohol, 90 percent or
    higher
glass container with a tight-fitting lid
spoon or stir stick
coffee filter
funnel
large bowl or tall bottle

METHOD

1. Add the turmeric and alcohol to the glass container and stir. Cover with the lid.

2. Let the mixture sit overnight, then shake vigorously.

3. Pour the liquid through a coffee filter over a large bowl, or alternatively, through a coffee filter–lined funnel into a tall bottle. Then, pour back into the glass container. This ink will keep pretty much forever due to the alcohol content. It does stain, so be careful in making and using.

VARIATIONS

This same recipe can be made using saffron. For a water-based ink, soak 1 tablespoon saffron in 2 cups (480 ml) water for several days until the water has turned a bright yellow. Discard the saffron bits and strain. For a slightly thicker, shinier ink, you can add a teaspoon shellac or gum arabic to the water as a binder.

Use: Alcohol-based inks work great in a blank marker and with other alcohol-based inks. They don't mix easily with water.

Suggested color pairings: Alcohol-based inks tend to repel water-based inks and refuse to mix. The effects can be interesting but difficult to work with, so I suggest making a range of alcohol-based colors to pair with your turmeric ink. Try using beets, iris petals, red peppers, or spinach leaves.

Other sources of yellow: Golden beets, saffron, goldenrod, annatto seeds, onion skins, tea, Osage orangewood chips, rhubarb roots, and butternut husks.

Note: A teaspoon of alum (a kind of aluminum salt found in the pickling or spice aisle of the grocery store) added to your boiling pot will intensify most plant-based yellow colors.

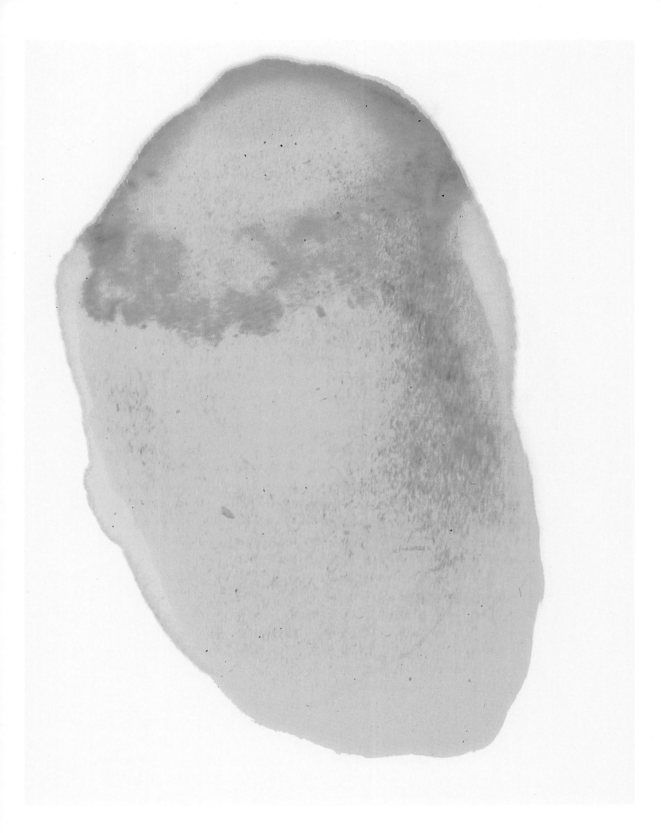

GRAY

Oak trees are incredible. They have been our oldest allies, providing us with strong timber for everything from Viking ships to the rafters of the debating chamber of the UK's House of Commons, from the sculptured arches of churches to fine wine barrels. Even earlier than all that, oak trees were a sustaining food source: Acorns, which were pulverized and washed to remove their bitterness, were used as flour or porridge. Our ancestors followed the growth of oak trees all across the world as the glaciers melted. I learned most of this from William Bryant Logan's book *Oak: The Frame of Civilization*, in which he also mentions that humans used oak to build Stonehenge, to create the first Stone Age–ending charcoal fuel, to make wagon wheels and sword handles, and to lay the first roads and build the first bridges. What better tree to mine for pigment?

There is of course, the jet-black oak gall ink (page 84), but oak galls can be difficult to come by. The common acorn is far more prevalent, and in my opinion, just as delightful. I was recently introduced to Japanese thread-spinning artist Hiroko Karuno, who dyes her handmade paper-based fibers a subtle silvery color that she calls "acorn cap gray." I wondered if I could make this same color as an ink. I tried fermenting the acorns in the backyard and then cooking them until I had a brownish water that smelled of dry leaves and forest floor. I filtered the ground acorns out of the water and further reduced the color bath to achieve an only slightly darker brown. Then I threw in a few rusty nails and a bedspring harvested from the streets of Brooklyn. The oxidized iron immediately darkened the water. I refiltered the ink and bottled it up. When I tested it on the page, I was thrilled to discover that as the water dried, the oxygen, iron, and tannins mingled to form a subtle wash that reminded me of the silvery rains of the Pacific Northwest.

A lot can be done with gray ink; it feathers, bleeds, layers, and clouds up on the page when used with a brush. With a dip pen it makes the perfect color of ink for a melancholy letter to a dying flame. Because no one should ever break up by text.

SILVERY ACORN CAP INK

COLLECTION

Acorns are plentiful in the fall. You can find them beneath oak trees, which are recognizable by their lobed leaves. There are quite a few varieties of oak; if anyone finds out the best one for acorn cap ink, please send me a letter.

MATERIALS

large, old pot
2 cups (455 g) washed acorn caps, plus more as
    needed
a few rusty nails or other rusty street finds, plus
    more as needed
fine-mesh strainer
coffee filter
funnel
glass container with a tight-fitting lid
paper, for testing
gum arabic
2-ounce glass bottle

METHOD

1. In a large, old pot, combine the acorn caps with 5 cups (1.2 L) water and the rusty nails or objects. Heat to boiling and boil for 2 hours, or until the liquid is reduced to about 2 cups (480 ml) of liquid.

2. Strain the resulting liquid, first through a fine-mesh strainer to remove large pieces, and then through a coffee filter–lined funnel into the glass container.

3. Test out the ink on paper. If you're looking to achieve a darker color, add the ink back to the pot with some more acorn caps and rust, and a bit more water as needed, then heat to boiling. When the ink reaches the desired color and consistency, refilter the result and add 10 drops of gum arabic for every 2-ounce (60 ml) bottle.

Use: This gray ink will darken on paper as it dries and mixes with oxygen. Give it time. Lay it on thick at night and see what it looks like the next day.

Suggested color pairings: Happily, gray goes great with all of the other recipes in this book, although it probably pairs best with an intense color like the magenta of pokeberry ink (see page 94) or the bright blue of copper oxide ink (see page 98).

Other sources of gray: Ground pencil lead, Canada thistle leaves, ground limestone, and mulberries.

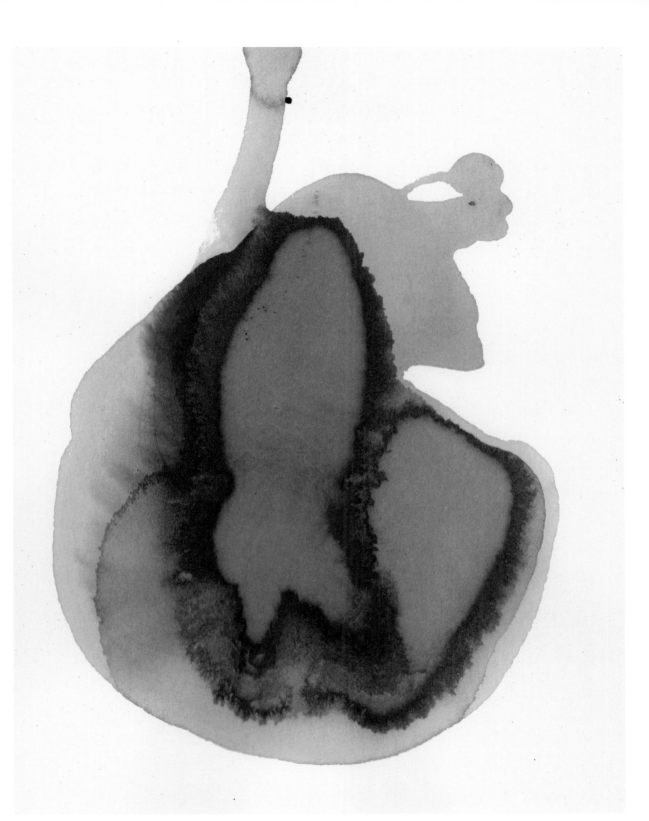

WHITE

"I have broken the blue boundary of color limits, come out into the white; beside me comrade-pilots swim in this infinity." —*Kazimir Malevich*, Suprematism

White ink is uncommon. On white paper it is counterintuitively light-absorbing—a watery, flowing contrast against the page. White paint, on the other hand, is dusty, chalky, and light-reflecting; it only shows up on colored paper. Plus, the only ancient recipes I could find for white pigment calls for a chunk of lead, steeped for weeks in vinegar under a bed of straw and manure until it develops a white crust, which even medieval colorists recognized as highly toxic. So why make white ink? My first answer is always, Why not? My second answer is: drywall. I have always been curious about the crumbled white bits of raw material sitting in renovation bins and construction sites across the city. Drywall is comprised of gypsum, sandwiched between two sheets of paper; it's easy to harvest and grind back down into a white usable powder. A little research shows that gypsum is a mineral that has been prized for its durability and ability to withstand heat. It has been a construction worker's staple going as far back as the building of the pyramids. It is hard and white for the same reason teeth, bones, and shells are: calcium. Without calcium there would be no chalk, plaster casts, white countertops, no fine Carrara marble for Michelangelo's *David*, and no snowy white ink. If you are worried about the chemical additives in drywall, you can grind down blackboard chalk or even use plaster dust (which are both slightly purer forms of the same basic ingredients) for this recipe.

GYPSUM WHITE INK

COLLECTION

I make my white ink with found bits of drywall from building sites and renovation dumpsters common in my neighborhood. But for a more natural ink, you can use white chalkboard chalk or any soft white rock (such as limestone), ground down to form a soft white dust.

MATERIALS

1 cup of crumbled drywall, white chalk, or white limestone
mortar and pestle
fine-mesh strainer
1 cup (235 ml) water
2 tablespoons gum arabic
glass surface and glass muller or palette spatula (optional)
funnel
glass container with a tight-fitting lid

METHOD

1. Grind the drywall in a mortar and pestle until you have a fairly fine dust. (If using limestone, you can rub two rocks together to harvest chalk dust if you are patient.)

2. Sift the dust through a fine-mesh strainer until you have a fine, soft powder.

3. On a glass surface with a glass muller or palette spatula, if using (or with a mortar and pestle, or by constantly stirring in the glass container), gradually combine drywall powder with water and gum arabic, a tablespoon of each ingredient at a time. Once they're fully integrated, you should have a liquid that's about the consistency of a strong espresso.

4. Funnel the ink into the glass container.

Use: This ink won't work in a pen, other than a feather quill, but it makes a beautiful, fine white line with a paintbrush on colored paper, or, with a thicker brush, a nice layered wash that is especially beautiful on gray or fawn-colored paper. You can add more water if it gets too thick to use.

Suggested color pairings: There is nothing more satisfying than white and black (pages 76–84) together on a page.

Other sources of white: The only other source of white that I know of is lead, and while the medieval recipe for lead white is fascinating and painters love it, it is highly toxic and not at all recommended.

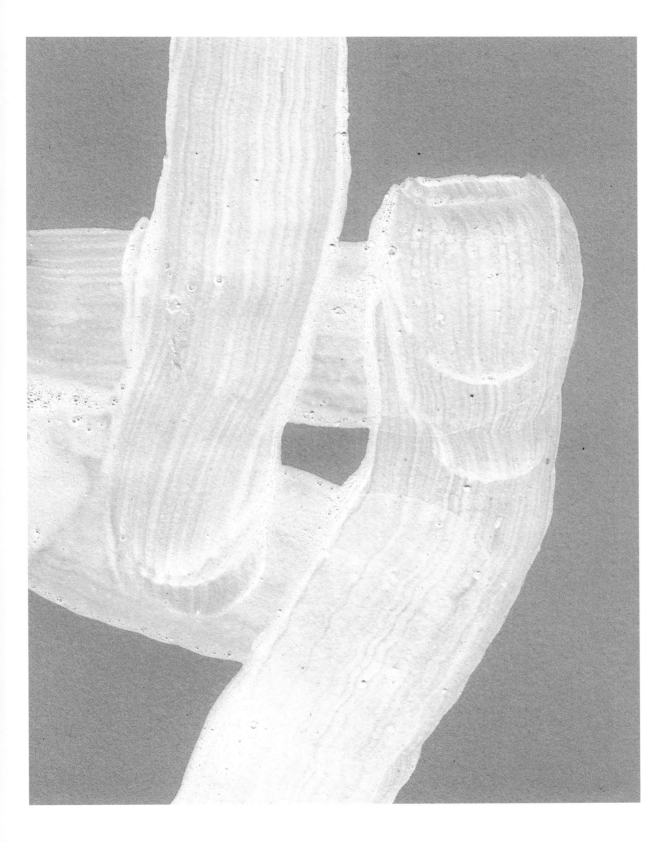

GREEN

"Green, how much I want you green." —Federico García Lorca, *"Somnambule Ballad"*

About fifteen minutes into my regular jogging route around High Park, by the southern edge of the duck pond, is a section of the paved path that's stained green and blue-gray with fallen berries. Above, the berries appear tightly clustered along the branches of a low shrub. In my experience, once you recognize buckthorn, it seems to be growing everywhere. An invasive species in North America, buckthorn is reviled by gardeners and arborists, and, in my local park, is ignored even by the birds despite its plentiful berries. Buckthorn comes from an interesting family. The alder buckthorn, considered the best wood for even-burning charcoal, is essential to the ballistics industry as a component of Swiss black gunpowder. But it is the common buckthorn and its berries that are particularly significant to the inkmaker. It's a tough plant, found mostly at the edges of swampy areas. Its inner bark is traditionally used to make a yellow dye, while its berries, round and small like currants, ripen to an almost purple-black color. By fall, they are plentiful and fat with juice that, once squeezed and filtered of its seeds, will produce a beautiful purple liquid. But this is still juice, not ink. Almost immediately the color begins to fade on paper, first to a dull violet and then to a shadowy gray.

My first thought was to try to intensify that rich purple by boiling it down, or to at least keep it from fading to gray by using some sort of stabilizer. But my research suggested that it is green, not purple, that famously comes from buckthorn berries. Sometimes known as French or Persian berries, they have a long history as an art and dyeing material. They were used in the yellowy greens of Vermeer and Rembrandt as a pigment called *stil de grain* yellow; they were also used in leather dyeing and for "sap green" ink found in medieval illuminated manuscripts. Sap green was one of the few medieval pigments sold in liquid form (it was carried around in a bladder). Despite the fact that the green of chlorophyll is everywhere in nature, it is a notoriously difficult color to achieve on paper. A sort of ink can be achieved by boiling down spinach or other really green leaves, but it pretty quickly fades to yellow. In the world of natural dyeing, a good green color most often comes from mixing colors, the most famous case of this being the green fabric produced in Lincoln and worn by Robin Hood's gang, which was made by over-dyeing with woad, a natural blue dye, and weld, a natural yellow dye.

The recipe for sap green is transformative, and it works something like magic. A drop of lye water added to purple buckthorn juice immediately shifts its color from purple to a rich blue, then, with another drop, to turquoise, then a bright green—and, if you add too much lye, a golden yellow, finally burning a hole in your paper if you let it. The transformation works because mildly corrosive lye raises the pH levels of the juice. The change is amazing to watch and the bright green, once stabilized, makes a beautiful and history-rich ink. It was buckthorn that forced me to relearn the pH scale. It was buckthorn that inspired me to cook up baking soda into soda ash, in my now obsessive quest to naturally tweak pH balance; it was buckthorn that taught me about anthocyanins and got me researching modern organic food coloring. Most significantly, it was this tenacious, overlooked shrub that taught me that color is alive, not just fading or darkening over time but sometimes moving across the spectrum.

SAP GREEN INK

COLLECTION

Buckthorn berries offer up their best pigments in the early fall, after the first frost, when they are fully ripened and black on the branches. I recommend collecting several batches worth so that you have enough to really test the color.

MATERIALS

large, old pot
4 cups (575 g) buckthorn berries
potato masher
fine-mesh strainer
large bowl
coffee filter
rubber gloves
½ teaspoon lye crystals
cold water
glass container with a tight-fitting lid
sticker paper, for labels
glass dropper
paper, for testing
gum arabic
2-ounce (60 ml) individual glass bottles

METHOD

1. In a large, old pot, crush the berries with a potato masher. Filter the mixture through a fine-mesh strainer with a bowl underneath to collect the liquid. Discard any solids. A further round of filtering the liquid through a coffee filter should give you a nice smooth juice.

2. While wearing rubber gloves, mix the lye crystals with the ½ cup (120 ml) water in one of the glass containers. Label this container "lye water" and keep out of reach of children and pets.

3. With a glass dropper, add one drop of the lye water at a time to the buckthorn juice until the color has changed from purple to green. Test out the color frequently on paper.

4. Pour ink into individual bottles. Add 10 drops of gum arabic to each 2-ounce bottle to create a slightly thick, glossy ink.

Use: Sap green ink can shift color depending on its pH, so you might need to adjust the ratio of lye water to buckthorn juice depending on the paper you are using.

Suggested color pairings: Sap green looks good with oak gall ink (page 84) or the bright magenta of pokeberry ink (page 94).

Other sources of green: Having found and perfected this recipe, there isn't much else that I like to use for green, although I have tried (with varying results) stinging nettle leaves, spinach leaves, grass, dock leaves, plantain roots, and broom stems.

Important Safety Note: This recipe involves lye, which is highly corrosive and potentially hazardous. Use caution and always wear rubber gloves when handling. Clean up any spills immediately using a water-soaked rag, which should then be safely discarded. Be sure to clearly label your lye solution and keep it out of reach of children and pets.

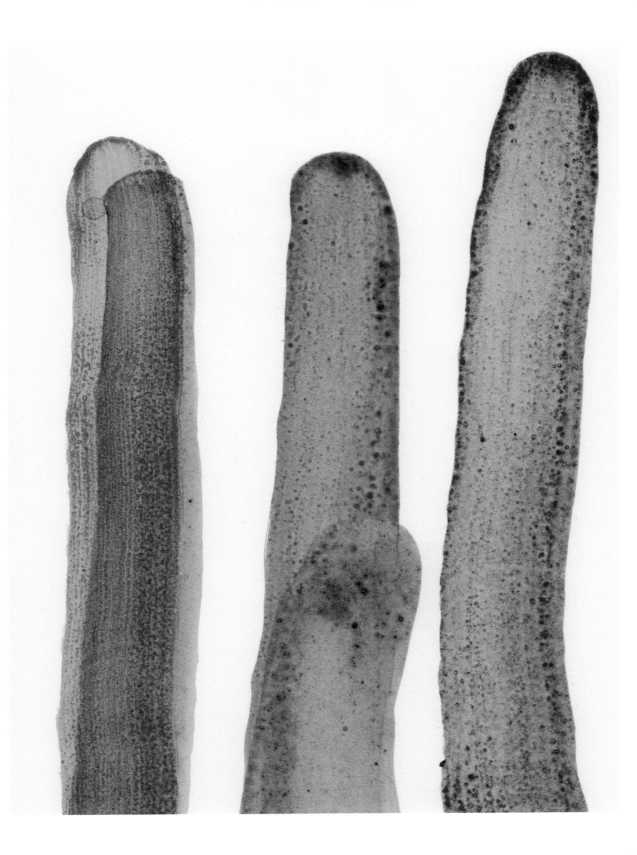

PINK

"Winter's breath is pink." —Sudeep Sen, *"Winter"*

A light, watery rose-petal color can be achieved by boiling sumac berries, rose hips, or the inner bark of the birch tree. Not surprisingly, the juice from cherries and raspberries can produce a temporary pink blush on paper. But for a darker, more permanent pink color, I recommend looking at dye recipes. Even with a more permanent formula, pink ink is usually only a wash, too frail for a pen or lettering. And yet it is irresistible. My favorite pink comes from safflower petals, whose yellow pigment transforms into pink as you modify your ink's pH. Safflowers are important in the history of color. A thistle-like annual bloom and one of humanity's oldest cultivated crops, safflowers were used as a dye for early Egyptian textiles and were found as decorative garlands in the tomb of Tutankhamun. They are also the origin of the phrase "red tape": cotton tape, dyed red with safflower, was once used to bundle government papers in Britain. You'll have to track down some litmus paper and soda ash (sold as washing soda)—or make your own (see Note)—and do a bit of work for this recipe, but the results are beautiful.

SAFFLOWER PINK INK

COLLECTION

Safflower petals should be harvested in early fall and dried. They tend to grow in an arid prairie environment and are harvested for their oil throughout the world. They can also be foraged from your local health food store or from the internet.

MATERIALS

large, old bowls or pots
3 cups (approx. 384 g) dried safflower petals
room-temperature water
large, flat spoon (optional)
1 tablespoon soda ash (see Note), plus more as
    needed
litmus paper
spoon or stir stick
paper, for testing
white vinegar
funnel
2-ounce (60 ml) individual glass bottles
gum arabic

Note: To make your own soda ash, preheat the oven to 200°F (90°C). Place a few tablespoons of baking soda on a baking sheet, and bake for
1 hour.

METHOD

1. In a large, old bowl or pot, soak the dried flowers in room-temperature water. Once the water turns bright yellow, discard the water and begin a second soaking with fresh water.

2. Continue soaking and discarding the water until the water stays clear. After the final soaking, squeeze as much of the water from the flowers as possible with your hands or by pressing down on

them with a large, flat spoon. Return the flowers to the empty bowl.

3. In a separate bowl, combine the soda ash with 2 cups (480 ml) room temperature water.

4. Check the pH of the water using litmus paper, stirring and adding more soda ash as needed until the solution is pH 11.

5. Add the soda ash solution to the bowl with the flowers and stir. Soak for 2 hours, or until the liquid creates a pink color on paper that you like (keep testing it by dipping a strip of regular paper into the liquid). Then add a few drops of vinegar.

6. Funnel the liquid into individual bottles. Add a few drops of gum arabic to each bottle.

Use: This is a light, delicate color that looks beautiful in layers. Its subtlety comes out in broad brushstrokes and large washes of color on paper.

Suggested color pairings: Pink and green have a satisfyingly retro, 1980s-preppy look. But pink is also beautiful with copper oxide ink (page 98), vine black ink (page 76), and silvery acorn cap ink (page 114).

Other sources of pink: Cherries, hibiscus flowers, rose hips, avocado pit and skin, bloodroot, and the inner bark of the birch tree.

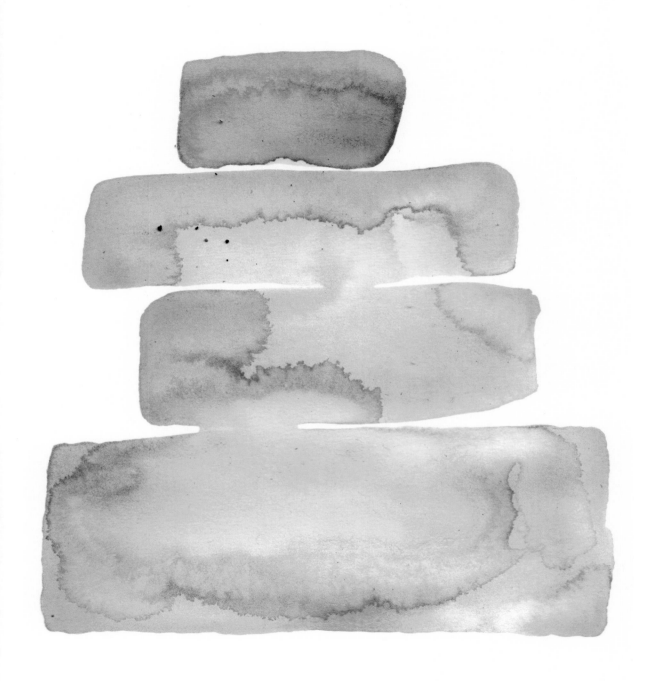

3.

TEST

INK

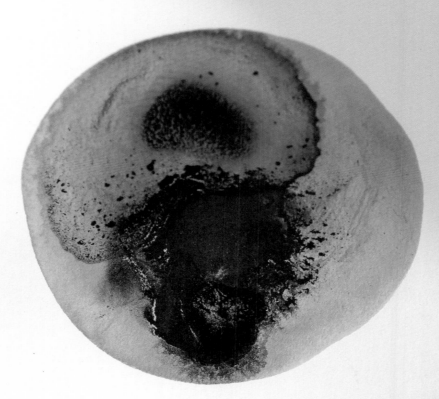

EASIER EACH TIME

TESTING INK ON PAPER

Paper is ink's sister. Unsurprisingly, the ancient civilizations of China and Egypt seemed to have invented paper around the same time that they invented ink. Today, Eastern papers are often sold in rolls and act more like textiles, soaking up ink and allowing it to spread and bleed in curious ways, whereas Western watercolor paper is "sized," which means its surface is treated with additives that fill pores and stiffen the paper, enabling the ink to sit on top of the paper and spread evenly across it. I love both but find the latter tends to reflect the whiteness of the paper, and in doing so, accentuates the mixing of colors in natural inks, as they react to each other on the page. For a more watery ink, however, there is something incredible about the way it can soak into and bleed across a fine Japanese handmade paper. The world of Japanese papers includes sizing as well as myriad textures, materials, and thicknesses that reward the explorer. The true tinkerer might also be drawn to making their own handmade paper as a medium for handmade ink.

For my ink tests I buy relatively inexpensive Stonehenge paper in large sheets and cut it down into squares. For a thicker, more archival-feeling paper I like Fabriano Artistico's 300 lb hot press variety. I like to start with a whole pile of paper as well as little scraps for dipping into the color bath.

When you are working with natural inks and you make something you love, you may want to spray it with a fixative. I recommend the all-natural, milk-based casein fixative called Spectrafix. If you don't want your work to fade or change with exposure, this fixative will archive it for you. It's also worthwhile to take pictures of your tests as they are changing to have a record of the way they looked at any given moment. Personally, I try not to worry about the image I am creating and just sit back and let the ink do its thing on paper. This is the best drug: Playing with ink is somehow exciting and calming at the same time. I like to start with my most watery ink and create a large pool into which I drop the more intense colors. I am sure you will find your own method and rhythms and aesthetics. This is an art, craft, and science that has endless possibilities and no wrong moves.

30 / 6	RAILPATH PALLET: ROSES, COPPERWIRE, WILLOW, DOCK

THE TORONTO INK COMPANY

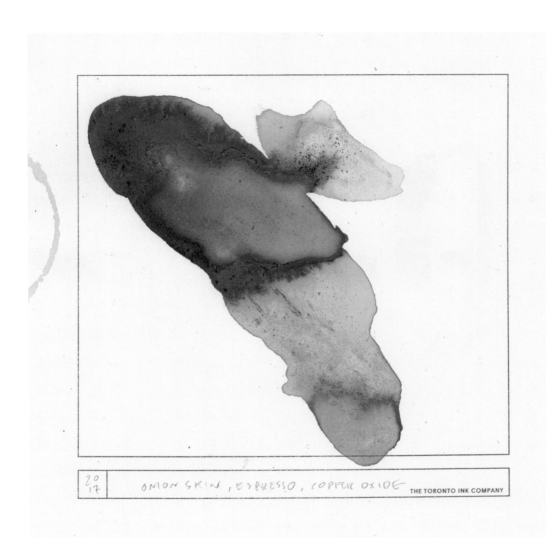

ONION SKIN, ESPRESSO, COPPER OXIDE

THE TORONTO INK COMPANY

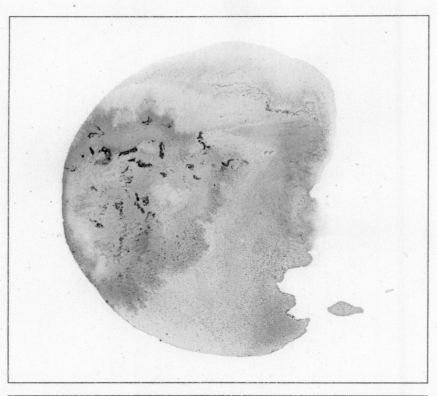

20
17   COPPER + RUST

THE TORONTO INK COMPANY

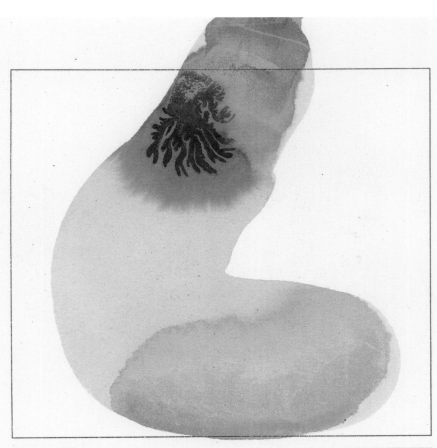

20.
16 (COPPER , TREE GUM , STINGING NETTLE (TORONTO ISLAND)
THE TORONTO INK COMPANY

20
16 CUTTLEFISH INK , COPPER, BLACK WALNUT , SALT
THE TORONTO INK COMPANY

20
16 COCHINEAL, TURMERIC ALCOHOL, ALUM   THE TORONTO INK COMPANY

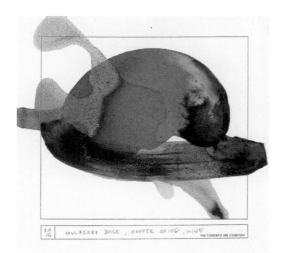

20/16   MULBERRY JUICE , COPPER OXIDE , WINE
THE TORONTO INK COMPANY

20/17   BLACK BEANS MULBERRY , SUMAC DUST , SHELLAC
THE TORONTO INK COMPANY

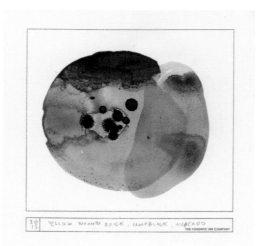

20/17   YELLOW TORONTO BRICK , LAMPBLACK , AVACADO
THE TORONTO INK COMPANY

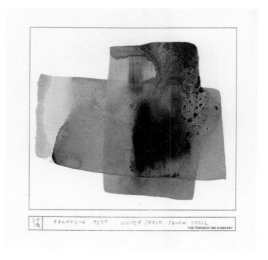

20/18   FRANKLIN TEST   LICHEN /ROCK /OVEN SHELL
THE TORONTO INK COMPANY

ACORN SILVER + IRON + SILVERBERRIES, TREE SAP · THE TORONTO INK COMPANY

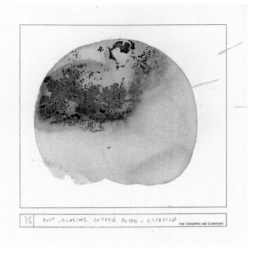

RUST, BLUEING COPPER OXIDE, ESPRESSO · THE TORONTO INK COMPANY

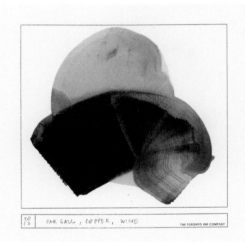

OAK GALL, COPPER, WINE · THE TORONTO INK COMPANY

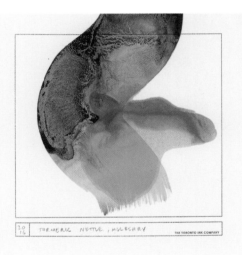

TURMERIC NETTLE, MULBERRY · THE TORONTO INK COMPANY

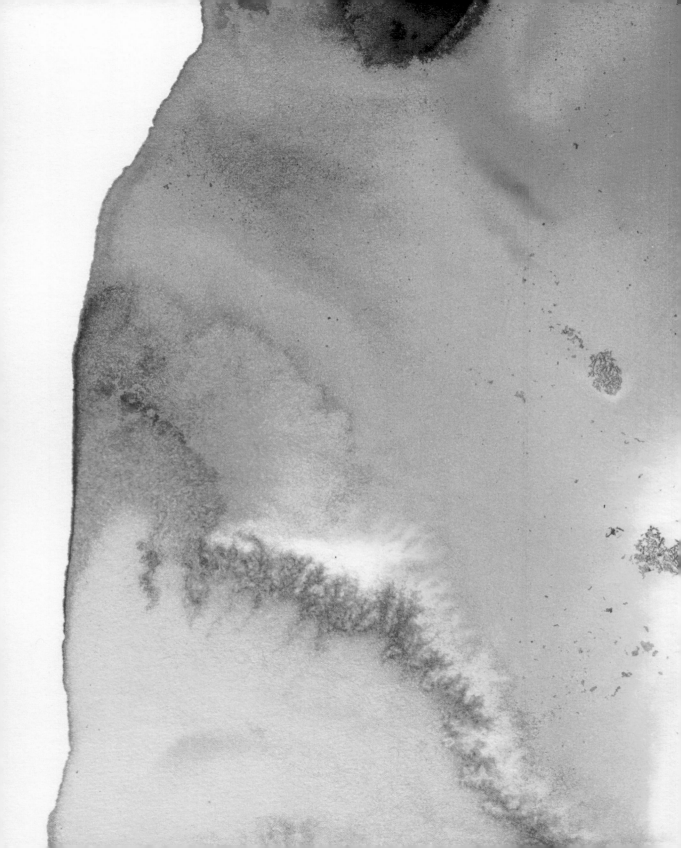

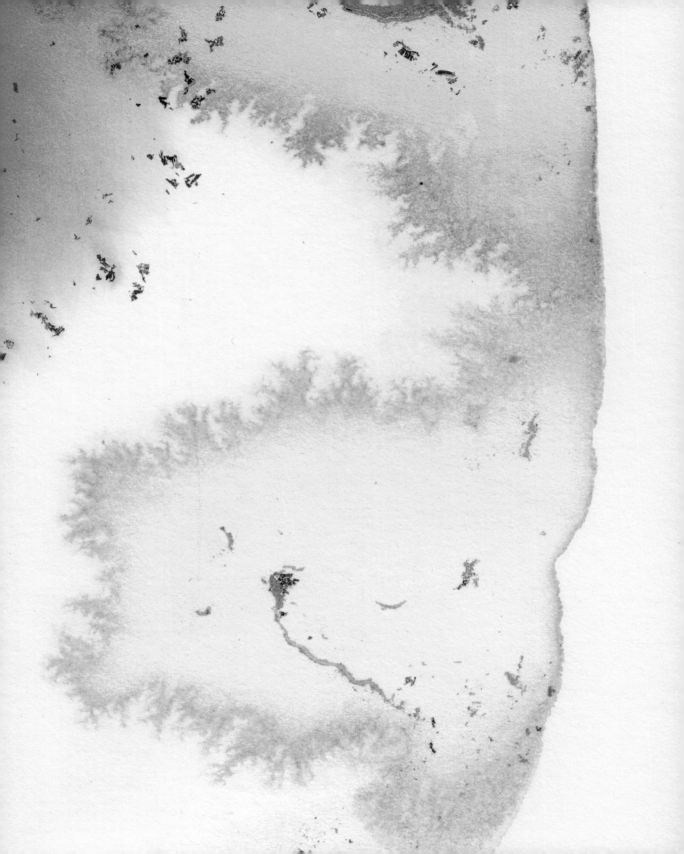

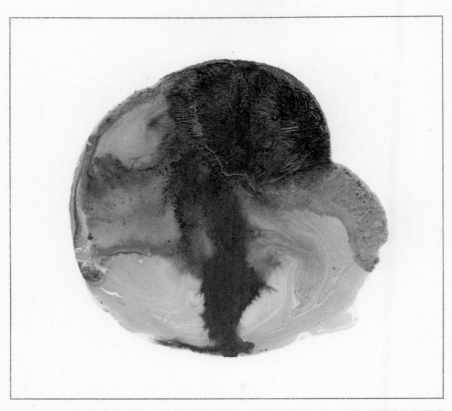

GOLDENROD, BIJLING, EPSON SALTS, COPPER

THE TORONTO INK COMPANY

20
17

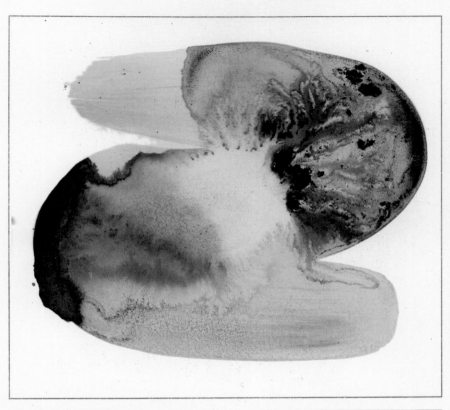

2017 'GRAPEVINE ASH , WILD GRAPE , GUM ARABIC

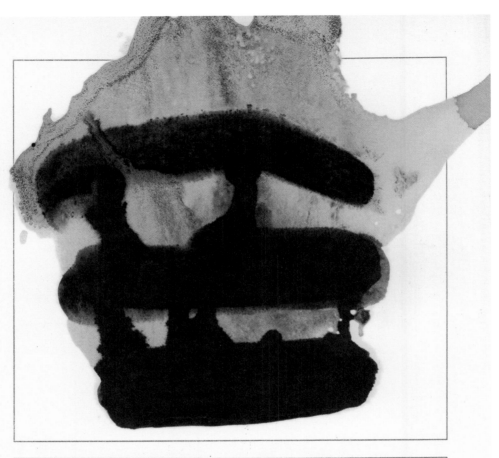

20 / 16   SQUID INK/GRAVE INK T BIRCH TEST A

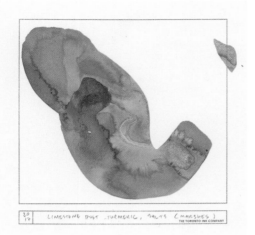

20/17 | LIMESTONE DUST, TURMERIC, SALTS (MARSHES)
THE TORONTO INK COMPANY

20/17 | HIBISCUS FLOWER, COCHINEAL, ALUM, LAMP BLACK
THE TORONTO INK COMPANY

20/17 | ACORN CAPS, IRON, FERROUS SULPHATE, COCHINEAL
THE TORONTO INK COMPANY

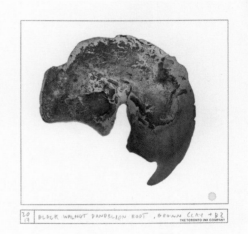

20/17 | BLACK WALNUT, DANDELION ROOT, BROWN CLAY + B2
THE TORONTO INK COMPANY

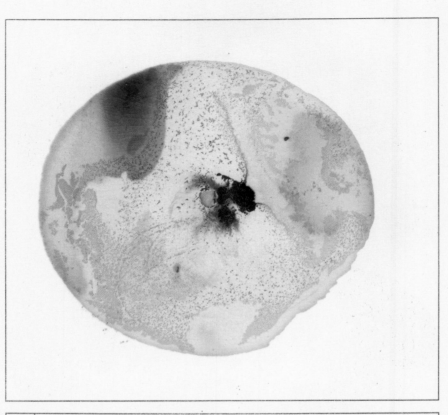

20/17   CHERRIES, LICHEN, SUMAC

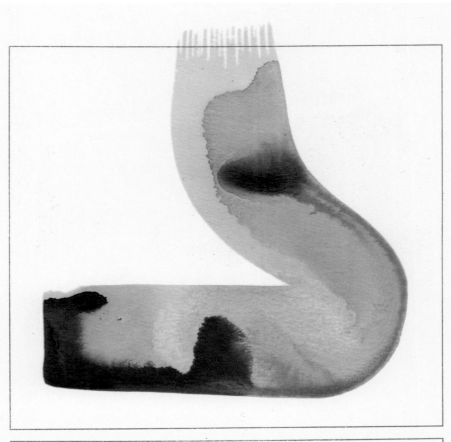

TURMERIC, VODKA, ACORN CAP, RUST

20
16

THE TORONTO INK COMPANY

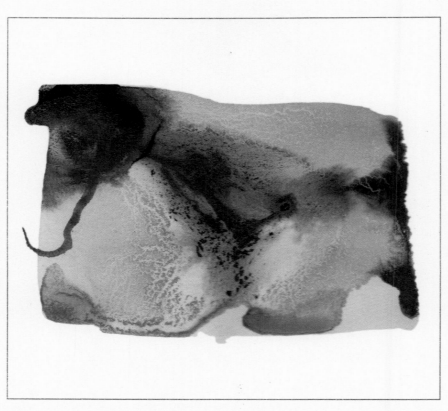

20 17	COPPER SALT, GRAPE SKIN	THE TORONTO INK COMPANY

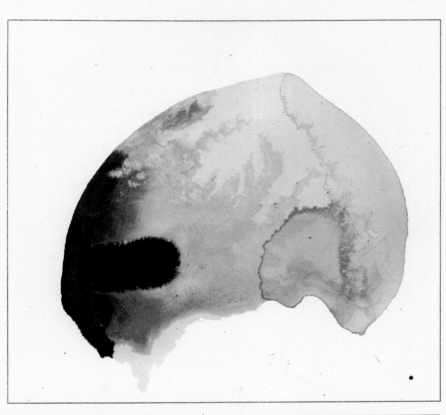

20
16 HOMEMADE PRUSSIAN BLUE , ROASTED CHICHORY COFFEE
THE TORONTO INK COMPANY

ON COLLABORATION WITH ARTISTS

Without a hand to guide it, ink is just colorful water. When I first started making my own ink with black walnuts, I bought a box of glass bottles, designed labels, and sent off a series of packages of carefully handmade, rich brown ink to all my favorite artists. A few of them sent me back artwork in the mail; a few sent me a note about how this art supply was working for them; a few posted their "tests" to Instagram. In fact, I find I am increasingly using Instagram as a collaboration tool. I call the people who use Toronto Ink "beta testers," as each bottle is a work in progress, and each person who uses this ink takes it further than it could ever go alone. Take, for example, beta tester Marta Alexandra Abbott, an artist based in Rome. While in residency in 2017 on Block Island, off the coast of Rhode Island, Marta collected seaweed that she then dipped in natural Toronto Ink Company pigments to create plant impressions—a triple collaboration between nature, artist, and inkmaker.

Kids are great beta testers, too, often ignoring the rules of art and craft and instead obeying the *un*-rules of pure experimentation and creativity. For this reason, some of my most important research happens at the level of workshops and pop-up ink factories, which allow participants to make their own ink while connecting to their immediate environs. These gatherings help me to define the direction of my company. In making this book, I sent out a bunch of packages to my ink heroes—people who have been pushing the potential of ink since before I started making it. This list of ink heroes necessarily includes novelists, poets, and illustrators alongside pure visual artists. Along the way, my packages of ink have even had their own adventures. Some of my test bottles of ink were stopped at customs, some languished on the desks of gallery assistants, and at least one bottle of wild grape ink almost exploded on its way to meet Stephen King. What follows is the work of just a small sampling of some of my favorite visual thinkers.

KAYO NOMURA
Toronto Inks mixed with watercolors

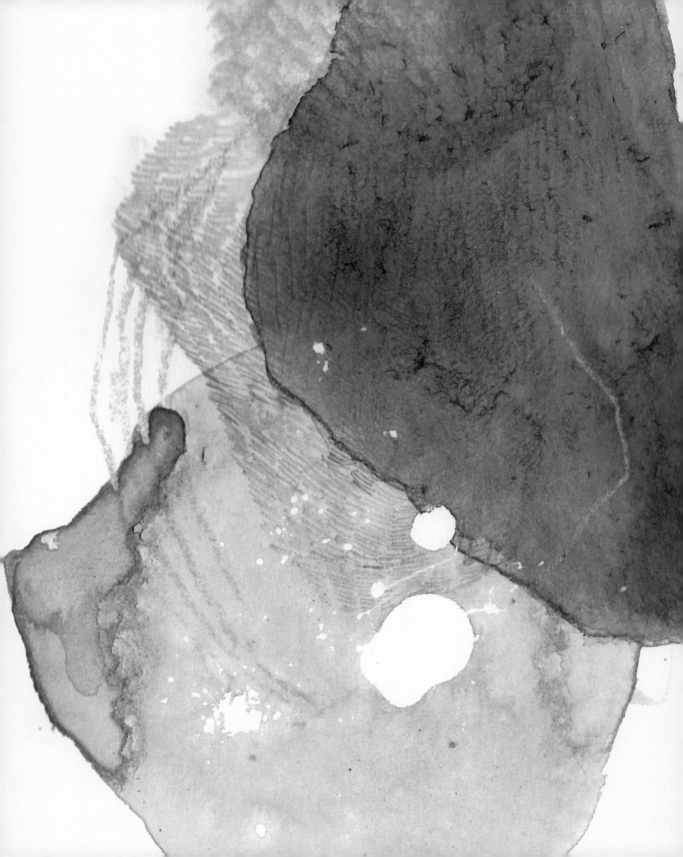

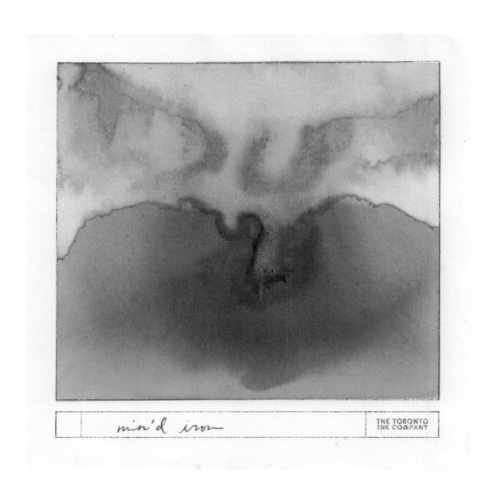

mined iron

THE TORONTO
INK COMPANY

HEIDI GUSTAFSON

Railway-Spike Rust

MARCEL DZAMA
Black Walnut,
Lye-Rich Sap Green

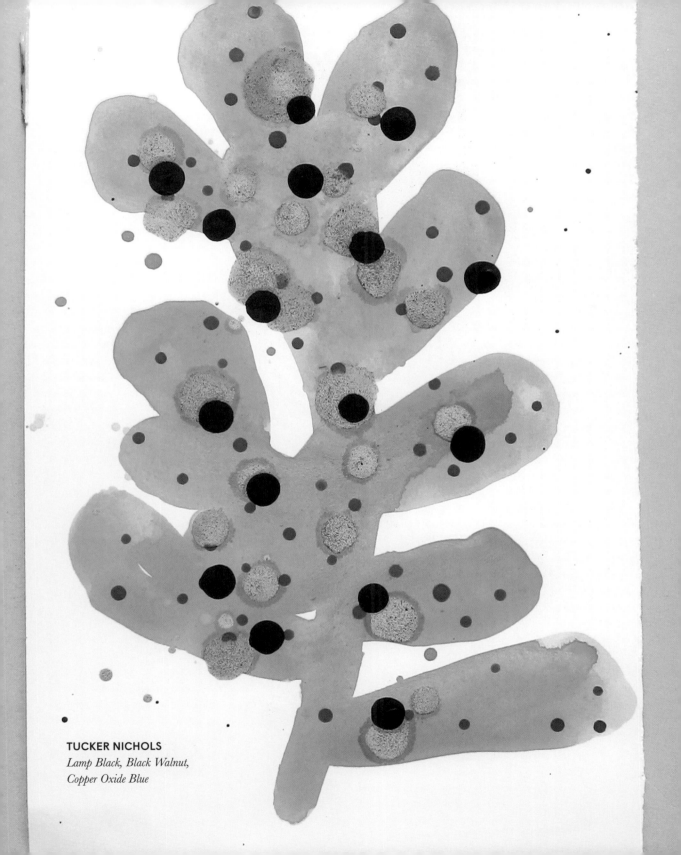

TUCKER NICHOLS
Lamp Black, Black Walnut,
Copper Oxide Blue

EDEL RODRIGUEZ

Sumac, Lamp Black,
Black Walnut

GARY TAXALI

Prussian Blue, Copper Oxide Blue
(both custom-made)

162

ANI CASTILLLO
Wild Grape

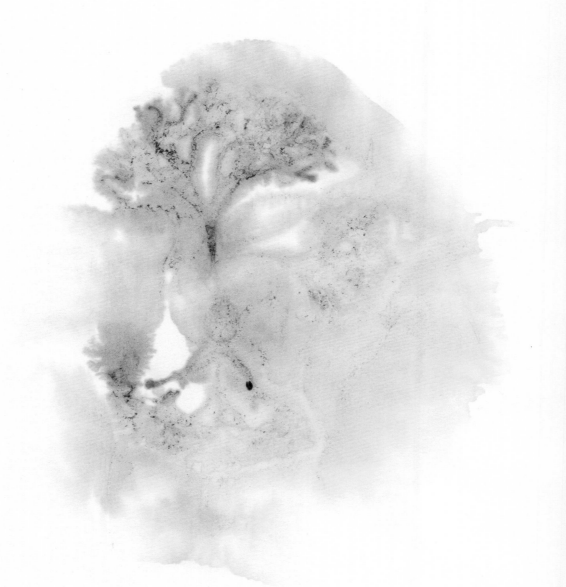

MARTA ABBOTT
Sumac (left)
Canadian Goldenrod (right)

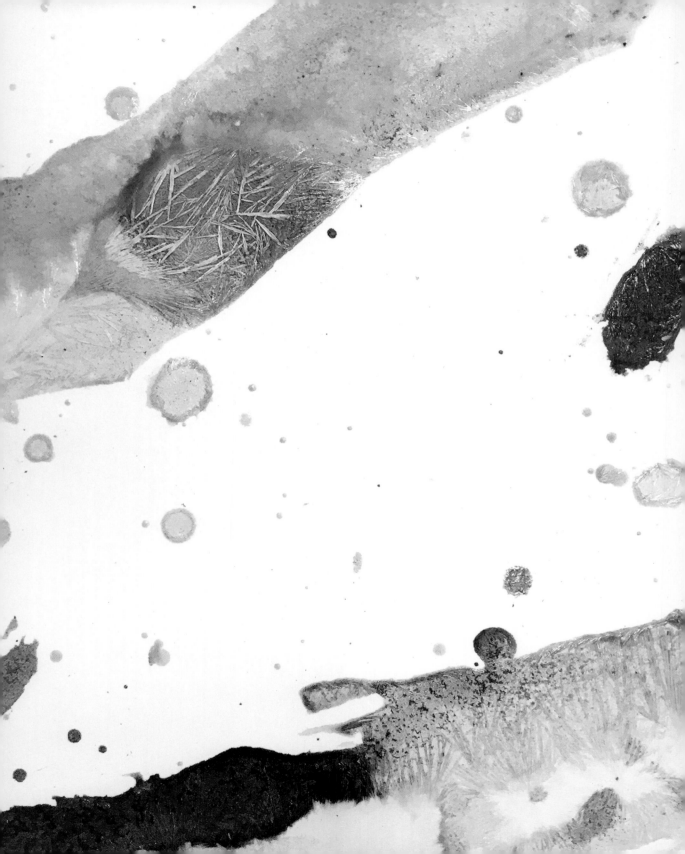

HIROAKI OOKA

Wild Grape, Buckthorn,
Rust (all custom-made)

LEANNE SHAPTON

Sap Green, Wild Grape,
Turmeric

JASON POLAN

Three-Borough Acorn Cap Gray

A
TOW TRUCK
PULLING
AN
AMBULANCE

TAMARA SHOPSIN 1/01/2018   THE TORONTO INK COMPANY

TAMARA SHOPSIN
Sap Green

HUGO GUINNESS

Gray Horsetail Ash

SETH

Oak Gall Prussian Blue (custom-made)

DAVE EGGERS

Sumac, Lamp Black

MARGARET ATWOOD

Wild Grape,
Lamp Black

CONVERSATION WITH MICHAEL ONDAATJE

MICHAEL ONDAATJE: When I was nine years old in a Sri Lankan boarding school, I decided to make ink, thinking I could make some money out of it. I bought, from some ancient shop, these ink tablets and filled a bathtub full of water and put the tablets in. I had more ink than I would ever need in my whole life. In any case, no one was interested in buying any of it, so it's strange that half a century or more later, I meet someone who actually makes ink. I'm just wondering if you had a kind of seminal moment in your youth where the future of ink turned up?

JASON LOGAN: When I was eighteen, I spent a couple months in a hospital where I couldn't eat anything, I couldn't do anything, I was just immobilized in bed with an IV, and someone gave me a sketch pad and I just started drawing and writing. I think ink for me has always been a connection between drawing and writing. When you write with ink it's very tight. It makes really fine, crisp lines, and then when you add water it becomes this sort of watery, wavery thing that's like drawing, and I love that you could do both. For me the physicality of ink started in my sketchbooks at maybe eighteen or nineteen.

MO: And that's also a thing that we can talk about now or even later on—the relationship between the word and drawing—or language and the sketch, and how they influence each other.

JL: I feel like every letter of every word is a little sketch of some kind. I think that words come at us first as an image and then we sort of decide what that image means. People talk about pictures and words as if they are separate things. I also spent so long in design and typography and I'm so aware of where letters curve and interact with each other.

MO: Were there books you remember that sort of blended these two things? Blended the act of language and the act of drawing? There was Kenneth Patchen's book of poetry called *The Journal of Albion Moonlight* that had lots of drawings in it. Or, more recently, something like John Berger's book *Bento's Sketchbook*, which is presented as a sketchbook, but it has his writing describing incidents and anecdotes, as well as his drawings. For someone like him, these two art forms are very, very close—these two languages really.

JL: I love the moment when writers go "I just have to sketch this right here," like in *The Little Prince*, when he draws the elephant inside the snake. There is no better way to do that then to draw your little picture right now.

MO: The poet Alice Oswald told me that she will do an abstract sketch on a page or two to try and discover the possible structure or plan of what she is going to write.

And just the other day I saw some of the letters of David Milne and other artists. Which are stunning, for a paragraph will be followed by a sketch of something he saw that morning, and then the sentences will continue. It felt to me like a perfect art form. It's the language of the drawing as well as the handwriting.

JL: It somehow adds to the personal urgency or something: "I am going to try to explain this to you in words—oh no, I need more than that—I can draw you a picture."

MO: It's not formal. It's a quick fragment, an aside.

JL: I love your word *fragment*. That piece of something left behind that is not the artwork or the finished form but something preparatory. Something that will fall away in the making. You have let me in on notebook first drafts of your novels, and the handwriting is beautifully illegible with various crossing-outs and colored boxes that only mean something to you, and yet I get a kind of meaning from them, a kind of energy. I find these scraps electrifying. I guess my question is, Why is the sketch so satisfying? And is the sketch just another part of the foraging process or a special thing of its own for you? Does it gain new meaning as a book becomes a complete thing for you?

MO: I am not sure if those are fragments or some subterranean plan that as an author I have not fully understood while using it. Like those abstract sketches by Alice Oswald. As in there is some buried map I am walking around in, not realizing it is Troy, or somewhere significant. I usually do not discover the real intent of the book until about three-quarters of the way into it. "Ah, so this is where I am going." So those early drafts are not so much sketches, but scraps. They may be questions to myself, or a clue. Sometimes I will glue a short poem by someone into the page of my exercise book where I am writing that has no connection to the work on the page. In a way, it is very much like your process of adding an element to the process of making an ink—a tone, a hint of X or Y that adds to the composition and color of an ink. But the look of those notebooks that have the first drafts—when I look back at them some years later when the book is over—still is a sort of mystery. It does not explain how the book was made or gathered. For me, in fact, the pleasure is in the curiosity of looking at them, the look of them. The process of the journey is still inarticulate. As you say, it reveals the energy. But it is almost as if it was not made by me.

JL: It's exciting. . . . Van Gogh's letters to his brother have beautiful little sketches.

MO: It would be nice to have such images like that in your book. It seems that there is some kind of twofold process here: I am mostly a writer and I would love to be able to draw, I'd love to be able to play the piano—those are crafts I don't feel like I can step into yet. Still, the kind of gathering of an idea, an emotion, or a feeling, or a sound when I am writing draws on them in some way. When I met you, I was meeting someone who was gathering and collecting and putting things together in much the same way, but to make an ink. It was completely fascinating to me. I hadn't even known ink could be made in such a way, except from those damn ink tablets I bought in Colombo. I hadn't known it had to do with collecting the ingredients. . . . So how does it begin?

JL: I think that things come out better when you forage first. I am loving all the fall foraging possibilities right now. If I have a full morning of

looking for wild grapes, say, and then a couple hours of mashing and distilling them, and boiling them up, and sterilizing the glass bottles and then sterilizing the little glass funnel and pouring it into the bottle and cutting my paper to exact sizes and adding a little stamp that says Toronto Ink Company, it is then—and only then—that I can begin. As a result, whatever I do, the mark is important because I know every piece that went into that mark.

MO: I wonder how different this is to writing. If I am writing something I don't really have that knowledge, or that intent, or even that understanding that something will be there when I finish it. So, maybe that process that you describe, the squashing of the grapes, the printing—all that stuff—for me actually happens when I'm actually writing, to discover whatever it is I'm writing about. Some writers know exactly what they are going to say beforehand, while I realize what the book is about as I approach the end. So the foraging for me happens in the very act of writing words down.

JL: I think there are two different pieces there, though. There are for me, anyway. There's the foraging, which is like, "Look, I need to do some research here. There are things I need in order to do this job." Then there's another kind of foraging as well, that's like, "I'm going to go out this morning, and I'm just going to . . ."

MO: Discover something.

JL: Yes, discover something and let things speak to me. I read that Guy Davenport book of essays that you recommended to me [*The Geography of the Imagination: Forty Essays*]. There is one essay at the very end on foraging. He used to go out with his family foraging for—

MO: Arrowheads.

JL: Yes, arrowheads. There's a great line in there where he says—near the end—"I learned from a whole childhood of looking in fields how the purpose of things ought perhaps to remain invisible, no more than half known. People who know exactly what they are doing seem to me to miss the vital part of any doing."

MO: Exactly!

JL: There is something so delicious about not knowing what you are doing. I love the, "I'm just going out." There is always something weird that happens.

MO: Very definitely. And that is one of the things that I admire about what you do. I mean I have seen you putting a mordant and various elements together. What is exciting about witnessing what you do is that kind of actual physical foraging—going out, finding "grape," this color of the grape or the color of some other herb. Can you talk a bit more about that? If not the pleasure, but the skill. Where do you forage, for instance?

JL: Well, the most promising stuff in the last few years has been these in-between places. Places where concrete and metal and building materials and old sidewalks meet grasses and weeds and vines. I just kind of like those areas. There is just sort of a part of me, a childlike glee, that's attracted to walking along a railroad track. But also, traditionally the best colors for dyes and for natural pigments have come from weeds, and weeds tend to grow in these out-of-the-way places in cities.

MO: Can I ask you why that is? Do you have any idea why the colors of weeds are more interesting?

JL: I feel like weeds are just tougher, I feel like they've got—they have had to solve more problems. There are a lot of weeds that are used for medicine, too. I met this doctor, who I love, who is sort of curing cancer with dandelion roots.

MO: Really?

JL: He really is. He was a chemist, and he has become an herbalist essentially, and he said that after thirty or forty years of chemistry, he realized that nature is the best chemist. It's been doing it over the last half a million years. These tough weeds have just figured out the answers to things, and one of the things they have figured out is how to intensify color. I am not even totally sure why weeds are often the best source of color, but they really are.

MO: Anyway, you were talking about the various places you go and find these things.

JL: The one thing is that I find the weeds in the sort of corner pockets of the city. Also in these pockets of the city are metals and industrial waste. When I started out with this inkmaking, I really wanted to do it all naturally. I wanted an art supply that I could cook up in my kitchen that I could use around the kids; as I started getting into it I found there were a lot of cool things you could do with metals that are not totally nontoxic or natural.

MO: Can you talk a bit about that?

JL: The most famous case is the oak gall ink, which is an ink made from these little oak apples or oak galls that form on oak trees where a wasp has laid her eggs; the interaction between the baby wasps and the tree creates this really intense tannic acid, which when mixed with iron makes a long-lasting ink—one that has been used for centuries, from around the birth of Christ to the present. A couple thousand years of the blackest, most archival ink. A classic case of metal interacting with nature. The result is this super velvety, beautiful black. But I've also started picking up pieces of copper wire and putting them in vinegar and watching them. The way that pennies get green, the copper wire becomes blueish green.

MO: Weren't you supposed to urinate on copper to make it green?

JL: You can urinate, too. Specifically for copper metal, the best is apple cider vinegar and a bit of salt; you get a beautiful greenish blue. It's the blueish green that's on the papyrus of the Dead Sea Scrolls. The Egyptians were using this same pigment—they mixed it with glass, actually. And when you see it, it has a kind of—it feels a bit Egyptian. It's a blue-green, with a slightly psychedelic, Egyptian gods feel to it. Very nice with black.

MO: So, there is this huge source in the world around us to make ink. It's not just one source—it seems to be everywhere in terms of what's available.

JL: I'd say yes and no. Sometimes I start telling people about ink and then they set out and every time they see something they smash it up and add water to it, and come back to me irritated it didn't make ink. I want to be careful with my proselytizing. I do feel like you can make color from anything, but there's a lot of things that look really colorful that produce zero color. I guess the quick answer is that there's an amazing amount of stuff in the world that can make ink and almost no one is making ink out of natural materials.

MO: If you are going to talk about ink in Japan, for instance, as opposed to ink in Europe or Germany, is it very different? Is it the same recipe or is it a whole different language?

JL: Well, modern Japan certainly makes a lot of beautiful pens, but there's a big split in Eastern and Western ink worlds. The main innovation that came from China and moved to Japan was just that ink is in a solid form.

MO: In China, originally?

JL: And still, in China. If you're a kid learning calligraphy you take your stone and some kind of ink stick and you rub the ink stick against the stone and you add a little bit of water. It's an amazing innovation because a big part of people's stories about ink are how they spilled ink on something and stained it forever. The innovation of the classic Chinese ink is to ask: Why not have it as a block so that you can drip as much water on it as you want? You become the maker of the ink.

MO: But that is for the paint brush?

JL: Yes, the brush. It's such a different relationship to everything because their letterforms are pictures, and everything is brushed and you're learning to be a painter as you are learning to communicate. Like you and I are interested in the relationship between words and painting and communication and art and all that, but for someone of any age and any interest in China or Japan, you would just be inherently learning art and writing at the same time. It's one. And the paper is—our paper is all about the ink sitting on top of it, it's crisp and clean, whereas the Japanese papers are soft and the ink actually slowly enters it, and the two join each other.

MO: So, as the main figure in the Toronto Ink Company, do you have contacts with places like Japan in terms of other artists and inkmakers? Has that happened, or does that interest you?

JL: Yes, there's almost no small-scale, naturally sourced inkmaking companies in the world. But there are lots of people in pockets all over the world who are experimenting with ink in different ways or with natural colors or with historical pigments. I think I told you, I'm so excited about this guy, Ooka of the Shadows. I'm saying "guy" but I'm not sure if they're male or female, but Ooka of the Shadows lives in a tiny village somewhere in Japan, and I send my ink to Ooka of the Shadows, and Ooka of the Shadows sends me back these ink-moving tools—different things he or she has built with bamboo and metal and things that he or she has carved, new ways of moving ink around. I feel like we are both inventing new forms for ink together. It's really exciting. Ooka of the Shadows just did a show of work. I made him or her a bunch of ink that crystallizes, that forms little crystals, and Ooka of the Shadows made an art show using those inks for the victims of the [2011 Tōhoku] tsunami, one of these little fishing villages that was almost totally wiped out by the tsunami. So, there's that person. Then there is this woman in Berlin I have this relationship with around distillation. She sends me—

MO: What do you mean by distillation?

JL: Well, a big part of inkmaking is that you take some color and you sort of distill it down. You intensify that color in some way and one of the ways to intensify color is that you let the water evaporate off and you get the color left over. She does these ink tests where it's just what's left over underneath the teacup—she'll have a date with a friend and she'll send me just the saucer from that date. So, I am working on what I can do with that.

MO: So, what most people don't realize is that there is a lot of mail going back and forth between these countries that's not the usual letter.

JL: That one was the flying saucer! It's so exciting to get stuff in the mail. There's another woman, named Heidi, who lives in the Pacific Northwest, who sends me these vials. She is only interested in iron. I send her iron water and iron-based ink and she sends me back these little vials of different colors of iron ore that are sort of pulverized down. I love the mail.

MO: There was something you said when we met recently. It was something about how important iron is in your craft. At first it seems like two totally different continents. One the liquid form, the other this basic hard metal. Can you talk a bit about that?

JL: I've been doing so much reading about iron. It's—I don't know where to start. On the human level, it was our first, as far as we know, ritualistic communication material. The very oldest examples of iron as a communication material can be found in caves in South Africa, and in those caves is this pulverized reddish rock, which has iron in it. Either it was used as face paint, or it was blown on the walls, or it was mixed with water to form some sort of paint. So, it's just this first way of striking out into the world as humans.

And if you look at the fact that most of Australia is iron—that iron-red—it makes sense that it played such a huge role for the first people there. And also, our first really good hard metal was iron. You think of the Iron Age—one of the first metal ages. And the very first real hard iron-based metals were made by the gods.

MO: Alchemy.

JL: Lightning hits the ground and fuses rock, and that rock became this thing that gets beaten into swords. Iron is such a—the iron plow has got a billion super-important human uses, but then it's a bit elemental that way. It's also so special because it really wants to give up electrons, in terms of its pure atomic chemistry. Iron is an element—from the periodic table—it's the element that wants to give away electrons and oxygen. Oxygen is the element that most wants to take on electrons, so the two of them have this amazing . . . marriage. It works for them, and it produces rust. I use rust for my ink because it's living, thriving, multicolored, multihued—rust is amazing.

MO: So does it survive in color?

JL: It really survives. It survives and changes. That's the other thing that makes my ink different than those evil corporate inks. It keeps changing. It's like a good vintage wine—you get a different one every year and not only that, it's going to change on the page, too.

MO: It will continue to change?

JL: Yes, it's alive. It's living, ink. I've got a few artists that use my inks. There's a guy in Scotland and someone in Poland and all over the world I have artists that love the textures and these subtle colors, and I just let them know it's totally not archival. You make a painting with this ink and I don't know how long it will last, and it might look different in a year. But I sort of like that.

MO: I remember you gave me a copy of one of these wonderful pages with three or four colors. There was a gray one, and I think you made those inks out of some ship?

JL: Oh, the *Franklin*.

MO: The *Franklin*. What exactly—how close to the ship did you get—what exactly did you make that out of?

JL: Well, that was almost like constructing a poem or a story or something. It was such a delicious project. I had an artist friend who was invited onto the *National Geographic* ships that were going up to the Arctic to study what was left of the Franklin expedition [the doomed 1845 British voyage to explore the Arctic led by Sir John Franklin]. Two ships went down [129 men were lost and the wreckage of the two ships was not discovered until 2014 and 2016].

MO: The *Terror* and the *Erebus* . . .

JL: Yes, the *Terror* and the *Erebus*. The guys all lost their minds. Some of them ate each other. There was spiral-shaped writing in a journal.

MO: Oh dear.

JL: The Inuit people up there had their own mythologies around it. A lot of our knowledge is from their stories about these ships. There was a whole problem with lead poisoning. They put everything in cans and there was all this British arrogance. There are about a million delicious pieces to it. In Greenwich, England, they have this museum dedicated to all the artifacts that have slowly come forth, and this friend of mine, who had been invited up on the *National Geographic* boat to write about it and draw some pictures of the artifacts, asked me if I could make some inks for her to use.

MO: So she stole some things from the ship? Some metal and wood?

JL: I created this series of about five inks. Lichen and rust, and bone and wood, and lead and quinine. I tried to choose what I saw as the elements of their world. Like, if they had had to make an ink, what could they have possibly made that ink out of? And some of them were kind of poetic. I turned the lead-poisoning theme into an ink. I ground up lead pencils, which made this beautiful silvery ink. And lichen. I collected a bunch of lichen from the oldest rocks in Canada. That's where urine comes back into the story, because the best color of lichen comes from prepubescent

boys' urine mixed with the far-north lichen that forms this kind of beautifully hued, really important color.

MO: Good God, who knew?

JL: I'm constantly entering into this weird, deep place—the internet is great for this type of thing. There's a long, elaborate story about the color yellow. India yellow. The rumor, which seems utterly impossible to dispel or accept, is that this intense yellow color that was used for hundreds of years in European painting is made when you force cows to eat mango leaves and their pee becomes this intensified version of the mango leaf, and then that is collected, dried, and formed into these little balls that get shipped off to the finest ateliers in Europe and made into paint. It's one of the great stories about color.

MO: Are there great shops in Paris or Bulgaria that sell ink? In Paris, I know of these art supply shops which I've been to that are wonderful.

I emailed you the other day because [my wife] Linda [Spalding, writer and editor] was trying to make some colors for wool. But when I see you making ink there is always something that you have to add to it, not to solidify it, but to make it work, and you use the word *mordant*, but what exactly is a mordant?

JL: It's the bite. I guess the bite is the thing. I've applied it to inkmaking, but it comes from dye and dyers' recipes: the idea that in order to make the color bite into the cloth—if you imagine this bunch of fluffy wool that you want the color to not just pass over but rather to grip onto—it takes some sort of mordant. Salts. Salt is a big one.

MO: When you put together your various recipes, when you are making inks, are you often surprised? Is the element of surprise something you wait for? Or, does it happen a lot? Or is it something that by now you know what is going to happen? Are there failures that lead to something interesting—an accident or something?

JL: When I say I love fermenting things in the

backyard, I have pots of things that go moldy and make no color—I feel like I'm constantly trying out new things that are not working at all. You must remember being a kid and mixing your paints. There's a certain point where it just becomes totally muddy. There's a point when it's really exciting and then it's, "Oh God."

MO: It goes too far.

JL: I feel like I have that a lot. I started painting on 16-mm film and got really excited by that. I had this beautiful old film of flowers blooming in fast motion, and I decided I was really into the metals and adding them to rust and copper and had the metals growing with the flowers. I didn't try it through a film projector, it was just beautiful to look at; each little frame was growing its own metal, and then the metal kept growing and just started eating through this celluloid and destroying it. I've had some really, really beautiful, important moments that have happened and then gone too far and can't be recorded in any way. I remember this specific one, this beaker. I had my headphones on, deep into the music, I had the beaker going. It was my very first experiment with making ink that crystallized, and I had my room all covered in the celluloid of the film, it was surrounding me and it was snowing outside, and I felt utterly encompassed by my own world. It was a project I'd been asked to do for someone. And I felt like a wizard. "I'm a wizard—I've been asked to do this—I'm utterly on my own, I'm utterly out there in some world, but I've been commissioned, I've been entrusted to do this," and there was something about the way it was snowing outside; I felt safe and warm yet weird at the same time.

MO: It was probably affecting you physically.

JL: I'm sure it was. I was shaking this tiny beaker —I'm really into medical glassware—and then the beaker broke, and I cut my hand, and I was there in my messy studio. It was sloppy. I remember so well the feeling of it all being right, and then the feeling of—what am I doing shaking this stupid beaker of yellow liquid. I feel like that's a really important part of the whole process, is feeling

ridiculous and then feeling excited that the thing that seemed ridiculous is actually sort of transcendent. And then it falls apart again.

MO: There's an old tradition of that. With your knowledge of nature around you here in Toronto, in Ontario, I wonder, are there other parts of the world you would specifically love to go to? For foraging? In North America or India or what? I'm just curious, if intellectually you think of a certain area of the world where you would love to gather some elements?

JL: The Middle East is really, really important for tree gums and saps and stuff like that. Something important happened between the way that ink and painting and pigments came together in human history. It was a trade between India and China, and then India and China and the Middle East, and then the Middle East and Europe—similar to the spice trade. For instance, the very best oak galls are called Aleppo oak galls, and they only come from Aleppo. There's Japan, which I'd love to go to. And I'd love to go to the salt mines of Poland. I feel like salt is a really, really special ingredient. It's up there with iron for me. Magical.

MO: The whole map-like sense of the moving cultures is very interesting: Middle East, Asia, China, and I guess eventually the Western world.

JL: The shellac that I buy comes from these little shellac beetles that come from a bush in the high mountains in India. Almost everything I make, I make from the streets of Toronto, except the shellac. I would like to at least meet those little beetles.

MO: The first creature that I remember very vividly is called the golden beetle in Sri Lanka. It was sacred.

JL: Beetles strangely play a really important role in pigment and ink.

MO: What other creatures?

JL: There's also those little beetles, or mites,

that live on the prickly pear cactus. They eat the purple—the magenta syrup of the prickly pear cactus. Mexico almost more than any other place is rich in color. There are parts of England, too. The English have this kind of satisfying, witchy relationship to all the herbs, and the dyeing of the wool. And then there's Italy.

MO: [*Laughs*]

JL: I mean I think there's two fantasy journeys to go on. One of them is to go find some of the sources, and the other one is to just go to a place where they've been making things with a very particular method for the last eight hundred years in the same way, and to really see that. I would love to get a bit exacting. Now that I know a few things about color, it would be nice to meet a real color master. I feel like I know a lot of obscure things but I don't feel like a craftsman at all. I'm more like a deep ink researcher. I would love to go to Florence and have the guy say, "Why are you grinding it in this clockwise motion?" I'd love to have my wrist slapped by some specifics of color manufacturing.

MO: We should plot about a journey. And find out where these professionals are, first of all. I remember being in India and going through whole villages where it was all about dyeing cloth. Fantastic fields of cloth to the horizon.

JL: There's saffron. Saffron is another one. Pollen from the tiny little flower. And when you get enough of it, it's this beautiful intense yellow.

MO: You have a sort of record of a lot of your work. You have your sketchbooks, which you've shown me over the last few years, pages and so forth. Can you talk about that? What is the process of that? It's kind of like a journal in a way.

JL: I really like to go to a place, and on my way back I make a postcard of that experience. It's almost like those things I make are little triggers to remind me of the place that I've gone to. They are not the place I've gone to, but they are more like the little marker on the way back. And, I've been heavily influenced by that quotation that you gave me—"following the brush." Sometimes I put those things on paper, and I sell them, and I put them up on the wall and they are beautiful in and of themselves, but they are not—they are not really art. They are not.

MO: Well they are, they are. What's nice is that you don't have to feel professional for something to be art. Things are art.

JL: I guess so. But maybe it's best to say that some of those things I do on the sheets of paper are a record.

MO: They are a record, but they are also an experience. They are evidence.

JL: *Evidence* is a great word.

MO: They are also stunningly beautiful. I think of your work as a map.

JL: Maybe *map* is a good word, too. The river is going to change, everything is going to change. The Earth is moving, the plates are moving—it's all moving, but at some point, the country was called this, and the border was here, and there was a mountain there. For me, at some point when the gypsum dust that I ground down from the drywall that I found near my house, when that hit this new liquid copper that I made, they came together and then they separated out. And that's something that happened once, that really did happen.

A TIMELINE OF INK

160 *million years ago* —— An inky ancestor of the modern cuttle fish first squirts out messages into the Atlantic Ocean.

40,000 *years ago* —— The earliest surviving record of color as communication (the grinding of iron-rich rocks into pigment) dates to this time. These first purposeful human markings were hand stencils—or what most first graders would know as "hand turkeys."

BCE

6500 —— Symbols dating from this time have been found on stones and turtle shells in the Henan province of China, pointing to the possible origins of written language.

3500 —— The height of cuneiform writing (little triangular stylus shapes punched into the soft clay of Mesopotamia and hardened into tablets).

3250 —— The approximate death date of Ötzi, whose remains were discovered in the Ötztal Alps in 1991. His mummy indicates that while he was alive, he received sixty-one inked tattoos across his body. It is speculated that these may have been administered as a kind of pain relief treatment, because these markings seem to align with injuries he sustained in his lifetime.

3200 —— The origins of Sumerian writing (historians say the first protowriting was mostly made by accountants).

3000 —— The earliest use of reed pens in Egypt.

2500 —— The earliest use of papyrus; Ink is independently invented in China and Egypt.

200–68 CE —— The Dead Sea Scrolls are created. Written with carbon black ink as well as with iron-based ink on parchment and papyrus, these were probably the most significant biblical find of the twentieth century and a victory for lasting black ink.

150 —— The first paper is used in China. The significance of this is worthy of its own book, but it would come to shape art, poetry, communication, and East-West relations in too many ways to count.

CE

79 —— A metal pen nib dating to this time was later found at Pompeii, along with a lot of ink, some great philosophy, and a few decent poems.

220 —— The first block printing in China (first on silk, and later on paper) is developed, setting off a revolution in communication comparable to the printing press in Europe.

380 —— Emperor Theodosius of Byzantium issues a decree forbidding the use of certain shades of purple except by the imperial family, on pain of death.

700 —— Quill pens replace reed pens in Europe.

953 —— The invention of the fountain pen is said to have occurred when the caliph of Egypt, Al-Mu'izz li-Dīn Allah, ordered the creation of a pen that would not stain his clothes or hands, thanks to self-contained ink in a small reservoir.

800–1500 —— The heyday of parchment made from animal skin—the fanciest version being vellum, which is made from calf skin. Also the heyday of feather quills (the best ones were made with the wing feathers of swans).

1040 —— Bi Sheng invents the first movable-type printing technology using ceramic materials and also wood, although the latter was later abandoned.

1403 —— Bronze movable type technology is first used in Korea.

1436–1450 —— Johannes Gutenberg develops the printing press.

1500 —— Oak gall inks made in monasteries are widely used.

1770s —— The earliest known use of glass ink bottles.

1828 —— John Mitchell in Birmingham, England, develops a machine-made steel pen point.

1856 —— William Henry Perkin, while seeking a cure for malaria, develops the first synthetic color, mauveine.

1884 —— Lewis Edson Waterman, an insurance broker, invents the first commercially made fountain pen.

1940s —— The modern version of the ballpoint pen is invented by Hungarian brothers László and György Bíró.

1970s —— The invention of inkjet printers.

1980–present —— The so-called death of print.

GLOSSARY OF TERMS

Below is a list of some of the concepts, tools, and ingredients that have proven important to me over time, and should start you off with a decent inkmaking vocabulary.

Alum

Alum (aluminum sulfate) is a naturally occurring basic mordant widely used in the ancient world and now easily found in the spice aisle. It will sometimes help berries retain a red hue on paper and can help natural yellow colors stay vibrant.

Aniline

Aniline dyes, or basic dyes, are a class of synthetic dyes originally derived from coal tar, first discovered in the nineteenth century. These dyes produce brilliant colors that work well on fabric and were a basis for early mass-produced pen inks. The first one was a purple called mauveine; it marked the beginning of the end for natural color.

Archil

Archil is a dye produced from the lichen *Roccella tinctoria*, which also produces cudbear and litmus. While lichen colors have been used for centuries to dye yarn, they represent (if harvested carefully) a huge avenue for the natural ink maker.

Binder

The glue that binds particles of color to water, or whatever your medium is. Binders also thicken and make ink shinier. Classic binders for ink include **gum arabic** and **shellac.**

Bleeding or bleedthrough

The effect of ink soaking through the paper so much that it crosses over to the other side of the page. Its less extreme form is called show-through or ghosting. For letter writers and pen specialists these symptoms can be problematic; for the experimental inkmaker they can lead to some interesting effects.

Casein

A natural protein obtained from cow's milk that produces a flat, water-resistant film. Because it dries hard and clear I like to use it as a natural alternative to the chemical fixatives used to protect artwork.

Cochineal

Cochineal (*Dactylopius coccus*) is the scale insect, native to Central and North America, from which the crimson-colored dye carmine is derived. Its history is a fascinating one, and the bright pinks it produces can make brilliant ink.

Dip pen

A type of nib pen with no ink reservoir. Natural inks often work best in a dip pen or glass pen, and depending on your recipe, can gum up an expensive fountain pen.

Fountain pen

A nib pen that contains a reservoir of ink.

Fugitive

Fugitive colors are prone to fading when exposed to sunlight (fugitive to light) or washing, as opposed to colorfast. Any natural ink may fade or change with exposure to light and oxygen. In some cases, a mordant or preservative may extend shelf life.

Gum arabic

Also known as acacia gum, gum arabic is a natural gum consisting of the hardened sap of various species of the acacia tree. It is edible and very useful in making natural ink. Most of it is harvested from wild trees in the Sudan.

Hull

The dry outer covering of a fruit, seed, or nut. In the black walnut, this is the green outer husk that encases the hard shell.

India ink

Ink that was traditionally made in China, it is composed of a fine soot that is combined with water and a binding agent such as shellac. This ink is more durable and permanent than fountain pen ink, but should only be reserved for use with dip pens.

Iron gall ink

A purple-black or brown-black ink made from iron salts and tannic acids. It was used for hundreds of years as the archival ink of choice but will eventually eat through most paper.

Lye

A strong alkali that is rich in potassium carbonate, lye is leached from wood ashes and used to raise pH in inkmaking and dye recipes.

Mordant

A mordant is a chemical used in combination with dye to affix the color to textile fibers. By using different mordants, dyers can often obtain a variety of colors and shades from the same dye. Because paper is made of tiny fibers, mordants are useful in ink recipes as well, as they can help color "bite" into paper.

Oak galls

Oak galls, nutgalls, or oak apples are a tannin-rich growth on oak trees produced when a wasp lays her eggs in the leaf buds of the tree. Oak galls can be used as a dye or a mordant, and are the key ingredient of **iron gall ink.** The best ones come from Aleppo, but they can be found on any oak tree.

Pigment

The "color" part of the ink, pigments are dry insoluble particles, usually pulverized, which, when suspended in a liquid **vehicle** or bound to water, form a paint, ink, or dye bath.

Shading

A common (and often desired) result of a fountain pen's ink pooling in certain parts of a letter when writing, with the color and saturation of the ink varying within a single letter or word. It's a characteristic that can't be achieved with a ballpoint pen, and adds to the subtlety and complexity of calligraphic and fountain pen letters.

Shellac

A yellow resin formed from the secretions of the lac insect, a beetle native to India and used in making varnish, India ink, and Sennelier brand inks.

Sizing

A coating for paper that affects its ability to absorb liquids (like ink). Heavily sized papers are typically more ideal for pens because they are smoother and more ink-repellant. Unsized paper can be interesting for testing the staining and bleeding effects of your inks.

Tannin

Tannin is an organic substance that is particularly intense in the nuts and bark of oak trees, the hulls of black walnut, and the leaves and stems of sumac trees. It is used as a **mordant** and darkens ink when mixed with iron.

Tyrian purple

Also known as royal purple, Tyrian purple is a purple-red dye that is extracted from the Mediterranean spiny deep sea murex snail. Murex dye was greatly prized in ancient times because it did not fade; rather, it became brighter and more intense with weathering and sunlight. It may also have been the source of purple ink used by Roman royalty.

Vehicle

The liquid component of an ink or paint. See **pigment**.

RESOURCES

USEFUL BOOKS

For individual ingredients, there is nothing better than a good old-fashioned internet search. Still, it's nice to have a library of reference texts. For a classic forager's guide to identifying different tree species, I recommend *Tree Finder: A Manual for Identification of Trees by Their Leaves* by May Theilgaard Watts. For a travelogue-meets-historical perspective, you might start with Ted Bishop's *The Social Life of Ink*. If you are a forager looking for color in nature, Jenny Dean's *Wild Color: The Complete Guide to Making and Using Natural Dyes* is a great starting point. If you just love the stories that surround the world of color, Victoria Finlay's *Colour: Travels Through the Paintbox* remains one of the best. *The Secret Lives of Color* by Kassia St. Clair includes even more stories in a kind of visual dictionary form. For a guide to lichen-based color, see *Lichen Dyes: The New Source Book* by Karen Diadick Casselman. For a broader guide to natural color, see Sasha Duerr's *Natural Color* and Kristine Vejar's *The Modern Natural Dyer*.

WHERE TO PURCHASE SUPPLIES

Really there is nothing in this book that can't be done in a small kitchen—with maybe a single trip to the art supply store for gum arabic. But as you get deeper into the traditions of inkmaking, you may find yourself looking for shops that sell more esoteric ingredients. My favorite two supply stores in Canada are: **Maiwa**, which focuses on natural dye methods and materials and includes a great selection of books, workshops, and information; and **Kama Pigments**, which is more of an artist's raw materials source based in Montreal. In Asia, **Pigment Tokyo** has an incredible showroom and some incredible Eastern ink materials, including fifty-year-old, aged inksticks available online. **Kremmer Pigments** based in Germany and New York is probably the best resource in the world for art and inkmaking supplies and workshops. **Sennelier** is a great source in France for fine and historical artmaking supplies and makes, in my opinion, the best commercial painting inks.

ACKNOWLEDGMENTS

There are a lot of ingredients that go into making a book about making ink. I will try to list them all, but forgive me if I've missed a step or two.

My first thanks has to be to my editor, creative director, and design guide, John Gall. Long before commissioning this book, Mr. Gall was a hero to me for his work as a book cover designer—in particular the butterfly specimen box covers for the Vladimir Nabokov series for Vintage Books. John miraculously recognized that there was a book in what I was up to in my studio and then guided me through this book with his light touch, intelligence, and patience.

My thanks go out to all of the Abrams staff who made this book possible, beautiful, spell-checked, and thoughtfully launched into the world, with a special thank you to Ashley Albert who helped me make sense without losing my voice, even into her Christmas holidays.

Next, the poet Mark Goldstein set me off on the right writing foot.

For the project with the *New York Times*, described in the introduction, I must thank Antonio DeLuca, Josephine Sedgewick, and the invaluable ethereal scouting advice of Krysti Keener.

Early on, Erika Oliveira talked me through recipes and books.

The novelist Heidi Sopinka and love of my life did some word magic to help my first writing connect feeling and sense. Already patient with my various adventures, she also put up with me through the making of the ink and the making of the book.

Then there was the Grey County ink artists residency sponsored by Clair Cameron.

First glance and ongoing support of the book came from my most trusted colleague, Angela Mullins.

My sort of secret creative director/influencer/gallerist Daniella Suppa gave me the most important advice of all, which was to enlist photographer Lauren Kolyn. Oh, Lauren. If this were an ink recipe, I would say Lauren was the water. Clear, beautiful, changing subtly with the weather, adept in both surface and depth: Lauren's photography, eye, and thinking binds this book together. In many ways, this is a photography book with a bit of writing alongside it.

My children, Kes, Soren, and Winter, deserve acknowledgment for their patience with me; they are collectors and inkmakers in their own right.

The book includes the work of a few of my ink heroes (to whom I owe a huge debt) but invisible here is a whole range of artists, experimenters, and workshop participants that have helped me define and refine my ink recipes and ideas. Stephen Herder has been particularly influential in helping me understand the role that chemistry plays in natural color and steering me in the direction of crystals and color. Ooka of the Shadows has provided me with tools that can be described only as made of bamboo and copper coming from the dream world. Another material-meets-spiritual expert, Heidi Gustafson, opened me up to the numinous aspects of iron. Kelly Tivan has focused my attention on the miracles of mirrors, condensation, and tea saucers. Marta Abott continues to reimagine what can be done with ink. Katie Bruce for her eyes, beautiful bruises, and support. Thanks also go out to Lisa Markon for her turmeric deliveries. Nancy Jacobi at the Japanese Paper Place for her entrepreneurial spirit and paper genius, Cristina Kerr at the McMichael Gallery for her support, and Canada's first indigenous printmaker, Anong Migwans Beams of Beams Paint, for her galactic inspiration. Michael Ondaatje for his ongoing interest and ear and guidance that just feels like friendship. The novelist Claudia Dey for setting up the card game.